The
BLACK
Presence
in the
BIBLE

Discovering THE BLACK and African identity of Biblical persons and nations.

Rev. Walter Arthur McCray

Volume 1
Teacher's Guide

General Introduction and In-depth Information

BLACK LIGHT FELLOWSHIP
Chicago, Illinois

Copy editor: Mary C. Lewis, *Chicago*

Cover Design: Troy Brown Design, *Chicago*

BLACK LIGHT FELLOWSHIP

P.O. Box 5369
Chicago, IL. 60680
2859 W. Wilcox St.
Chicago, IL. 60612

312.722.1441

ISBN: 0-933176-12-0

Library of Congress Catalog Card Number:
90-80108

Manufactured in the United States of America.

Dedication

To

ROSITA E. McCLAIN

my administrative assistant.

In her merciful, cheerful and energetic way
she has done more for the
Black presence in the Bible
than most people who know her
will ever realize this side of heaven.

The BLACK Presence in the BIBLE

Discovering THE BLACK and African identity of Biblical persons and nations.

Rev. Walter Arthur McCray

Volume 1
Teacher's Guide

General Introduction and In-depth Information

Books by Rev. Walter Arthur McCray

The Black Presence in the Bible *(Teacher's Guide)*
Discovering the Black and African Identity
    of Biblical Persons and Nations (1990)

**The Black Presence in the Bible and the Table of Nations
    (Genesis 10:1-32)**
With emphasis on the Hamitic Genealogical Line
    from a Black perspective (1990)

Black Folks and Christian Liberty
Be Christian. Be Black. Be Culturally and Socially Free!
    (1979, 1987)

Toward a Wholistic Liberation of Black People
Its Meaning as Expressed in the Objectives of
    the National Black Christian Students Conference (1979)

Saving the Black Marriage
Nine vital lessons on Settling, Saving,
    and Solidifying the Black Marriage (1981)

How to Stick Together during Times of Tension
Directives in Christian Black Unity (1983)

A Rationale for Christian Black Literature (1985)

Reaching and Teaching Black Young Adults
An exposition toward strengthening the Church through
    ministry to urban Black young adults. (1986)

The
BLACK
Presence
in the
BIBLE

D iscovering THE BLACK and African identity of Biblical persons and nations.

Rev. Walter Arthur McCray

Table of Contents

Charts, Illustrations, & Scripture Passages

Charts, Illustrations, & Scripture Passages *(cont.)*

Maps

Preface

What began in 1973 as a Bible study presentation to a group of undergraduate students, has now taken its present form: "The Black Presence in the Bible."

The motivation for the study at that time (a study entitled "Scriptural Attitudes Toward Cultural Differences") was to correct racist attitudes which white Christian students manifested toward their fellow Black students and Black people in general. The urgency this time is foremost to educate and inspire Black Christians and people everywhere by placing at their availability this vital and growing body of information.

Back then, the aim was to uncover the hypocritical inconsistencies of white Christians who claimed to love God and His Word, while at the same time they mistreated Black people whom God so identified, accepted and redeemed, as is adequately revealed in His Word! Presently, the aim is to affirm Black people in their God-given ethnic, cultural and personal distinctives, and to challenge them to reach the heights of their past and to claim the promises of their future as revealed in the Holy Scripture.

More and more people are becoming aware of the presence of Black people in Biblical history. Hopefully, these few pages will confirm in writing what many have already heard through the "grapevine." Namely, that a significant number of Black, that is African, people are noted in the Scripture.

The color and beauty of these Black persons is naturally accepted, the land from which they came is a point of reference, their history is remembered, their contributions are noted, their failures are described, and their future is prophesied. These Black persons were part of the community of faith in both the Old and New Testaments. They were respected and redeemed by God. And both individually and collectively, they played an important part in God's plan and work of salvation for the world.

This is not the first word on the subject of Black people in the Bible. Others have presented similar information through lecture, audio-visual means, and in print.[1] The author owes a great debt to Dr. Charles B. Copher (Atlanta, GA). It has been through several of his writings and many consultative conversations that I have been provided with a more solid basis from which the information in these pages could be presented. In several ways I have sought to build upon the foundation laid by this eminent Black Old Testament scholar, despite the reality that in certain dimensions of this study we hold highly contrasting views in our hermeneutical orientation, and in our sincere approach toward explaining several passages of Scripture. Albeit, despite our theological and historical divergences when it comes down to contextualizing the specific identification of some persons/people who Biblically may be classified as Black, we share a very great degree of unanimity. Over the past several years Dr. Copher and I have discovered enough brotherly love, tolerance, and commitment to the same Christian Black agenda to lecture in tandem on this subject which is so essential to the development and liberation of African peoples everywhere.[2]

The in-depth seminars in Chicago and across the country which the author has given on the fact and significance of the Bible's Black presence have contributed signficantly to the development of this material. Our interaction with wide-ranging audiences has helped to focus our presentation of the subject. At this juncture we feel the time is opportune for putting this significant information into its present form.

Any Biblical student seeking to do his/her own exegesis and exposition of the Scripture ought to be tremendously grateful to the growing number of Black scholars who have and are providing first-hand research, exceptional documentation, revisionist views, and creative insights into the study of ancient Black peoples. In many ways their studies directly impact our understanding of the Biblical context and message. To mention a few names, there are the works of Yosef A. A. ben-jochannan, James Brunson, John Henrik Clarke, Charles Copher, Cheikh Anta Diop, Cain Hope Felder, Charles S. Finch, William Leo Hansberry, Asa G. Hilliard, John G. Jackson, III, Drusilla Dunjee Houston, Runoko Rashidi, J. A. Rogers, Ivan Van Sertima, and Frank M. Snowden.

These and other Black scholars have **done their homework,** and in the process have sent many white historians and Biblical-historical theologians back to school. The studies of these scholars have yielded, from an essential Black perspective, the raw materials about the lands and indigenous peoples of the Biblical world needed to correct Biblically racist views and explanations. To be sure, not all these scholars agree on all points, and neither are all their conclusions tenable with regard to Christian faith and teachings. Yet, taken together, their collective thought is substantial. It would appear that the endeavors of the Black theologian who would do his own Biblical-historical investigation of the Scriptural text has been served well by his Black colleagues who, ipso facto, are providing us a Black apologetic in Biblical research.

We believe that this present treatment of the Black presence in the Bible offers a fresh perspective for a growing constituency of Christian Black educators and learners who seek to maintain a good respect for reliable Biblical and historical information. In style we have sought to take scholarly material and make it intellectually digestible to the common reader. Those who are teachers should discover quickly how easily they can grasp and share this message with their learners. Also, we have provided enough substantial content and resource leads (by the documentation provided in the endnotes and bibliography) so that the reader/teacher who desires may immediately plunge himself or herself into this inspiring, cleansing and therapeutic river of Black Biblical awareness.

Perhaps one of the more significant contributions this writing makes to the subject at hand, amidst a growing body of information, has been the attention the author has given to the philosophy of approach and structure in the identification process. Far too often we have witnessed spirited proponents of the Biblical Black presence proclaim the Blackness of a given character or people without providing the necessary tools and information for their listeners/readers to evaluate their claims. Our approach is different.

In addition to identifying numerous Black persons and nations, we have given consideration to such topics as: "Approach to Sources," "Why we speak of 'Black and African'," "The Definition of Blackness," "Ways for Identifying Black People," "From the Obvious to the More Difficult," "An Old Testament Time Line," etc. The reader is also provided with a somewhat detailed analysis of

Genesis 10, known as "The Table of Nations." This one passage of Scripture is foundational to our study, and the way it is viewed by the learner will do more to shape his/her findings than perhaps any other Biblical passages. The complementary volume to the one at hand is entitled: **The Black Presence in the Bible and the Table of Nations (Genesis 10:1-32): with emphasis on the Hamitic Genealogical Line from a Black Perspective.** Our readers are referred to it for a penetrating analysis of the Table.

In the appendix entitled "How to Begin the Discovery Process," the reader is led step by step in the use of research tools and a simple method of investigation which are accessible to the average Bible reader. Our aim in forming our treatment of this study in such a fashion has been, not to merely give the reader a fish, but to teach the reader how both to qualify the fish received and to cast his/her own net into the sea of Biblical Blackness.[3]

This meager treatment is only the beginning. Our priorities at this time permit us to produce only these few pages. However, we would hope that such a brief treatment of this very important subject will not render it a disservice. Nevertheless, we take the risk. The time to get the word out is now. The author assumes full responsibility for all errata appearing in this publication's final form. Where repetition occurs it is used for emphasis. We're doing the best we can with what we've got!

The present format of this material should lend itself to the reading of a wide audience who long for good, simple, and sound information at an affordable price! It is hoped this book will meet the need and in so doing quench the soul-thirst of millions of Black people grasping to locate their historical, ethnic, spiritual and personal roots and identity within the redemptive work of God through Christ Jesus revealed in His Word.

The author owes a great deal of gratitude to Reverend Dr. Charles B. Copher who critically read the manuscript, to Mary C. Lewis our copy editor, to Rosita E. McClain my administrative assistant, and to several others who supported and prayed for this work. My wife Thelma made a very special sacrifice. May the good Lord continue to bless and enrich her.

Reverend Walter Arthur McCray

xii.

SECTION I

Definitions and Terminology

A. Black Peoples are Written about in the Bible

B. Approach to Sources for the Study

C. Why We Speak of "Black and African"

D. The Definition of Blackness Used in the Study

E. The Bible's Explicit, Implicit, and Presumed

   Black Presence

F. The Transformation of Black Identity

A.

Black Peoples are Written about in the Bible

In a survey entitled "Three Thousand Years of Biblical Interpretation with Reference to Black Peoples" Dr. Charles B. Copher, a Black American, eminent and distinguished Old Testament scholar, has stated

> Granted that the Bible, along with interpretations of it, have proved to be and continue to be sources of blessings to millions of people. It is also true that these have been and continue to be sources of some of the greatest curses humankind has known...In no instance...has the Bible and interpretations of it led to such murder – physical, psychological, social, and spiritual – as in the case of Black people...such murder goes back to ancient times and is still being committed today.[4]

It has been the misuse of the Bible and the erroneous "interpretations" of men which provided the cesspool of so-called curses and actual murder upon Black humanity which Dr. Copher has disclosed in his survey.

An excellent case can be made for the argument that it has been Biblical "theologians" who were unenlightened by the Spirit of God – **Who is the Biblical Interpreter of the highest magnitude** – who are the perpetuators of this "blasphemy."[5] Further, abusive explanations and applications of the Scripture – especially, but by no means exclusively, with regard to Black people, stem from both a depraved heart and poor scholarship manifested in an ignorance of Biblical data. **What the Bible text says about Black people**, must always precede **what the Bible text means by what it says about Black people.** Let us be reminded that Jesus said "You are wrong, because you know neither the scriptures nor the power of God" (Matthew 22:29).

It is the position of the author that Black peoples are written about in the Bible. Elucidating and expounding this Black Biblical content is the thrust of this discourse.

The Bible we refer to, and which sets the parameters of our study, is the Sacred writings (Holy Scriptures) of the Judeo-Christian-Protestant tradition which have come down to us in the 66-book canon. By faith, those of us who are Christians accept these sacred writings as the Word of God revealed and addressed to humanity with a thrust of redemption and with Christ Jesus, the very deity of God, as its central Person and theme.[6]

The existence and experiences of ancient Black/African people are recorded in the Bible. The Bible contains a substantial amount of information written by Black people, about them, and, in many cases, is addressed specifically to them. Our quest is to uncover, understand, and exploit for righteous purposes this vital Biblical information about Black/African humanity.

B.

Approach to Sources for the Study

On one occasion when the author was presenting a seminar on the presence of Black people in the Biblical world, one of the persons attending made the following remark: "Why can't we just study the Bible and leave the other alone?" It was clear from her question that the limited perspective this sister espoused envisioned a kind of Bible study which was void of historical, cultural and ethnological information. To her, any study of the Scripture which led to the ethnic identification of the characters under consideration, particularly of Black peoples, was deemed non-Biblical and was therefore to be disregarded as anti-Christian! Our reply to our sister's question was quite simple: "We are *studying the Bible*."

We mention this experience for the following reason. Some of our less enlightened brothers and sisters (the sister asking the question was a Black American and a Christian), think that we are talking about other "books" and information when we study about Black people in the Scriptures: even though our seminars are entitled "The Black Presence in the **Bible**"! Some Black persons are so anti-Black and so unaware of their self-denigrating attitudes that they cannot see the obvious due to their prejudices.

In our effort to clearly show how we approach the study of this subject, we find it necessary to disclose the sources from which we draw our information. This disclosure should satisfy those who are Christian and/or who are honest searchers for truth.

The sources for the study of the Black presence in the Bible are three-fold. We use, first of all and essentially, the **Bible**, then **Bible reference books**, and finally **extra-biblical writings**.

1. The Bible

In uncovering the historical Black presence in the Scripture, **the Bible itself will be the primary source to inform this study.** We use the Bible because the Bible is the context of our study. The Bible we use is the same Bible which is commonly used by millions of Christians. It is composed of the 66 books of the Judeo-Christian-Protestant tradition. These sacred writings are composed of 39 books in the Old Testament and 27 books in the New Testament.

A number of modern and popular versions have been translated from the original Biblical Hebrew and Greek languages in which the Bible was written into English. These versions include the *New Revised Standard Version* (NRSV), the *New International Version* (NIV), the *Revised Standard Version* (RSV), the *New American Standard Version* (NASV), *Today's English Version* (TEV, *"The Good News Bible"*), and of course, the older and traditional *King James Version* (KJV, or *Authorized Version* (AV)). All of these translations are good to use for study. All are the Bible.

Of course, if one has a good working knowledge of the Biblical languages, Hebrew in the Old Testament and Greek in the New Testament, he/she is encouraged to make use of them when studying this subject.

The author approaches the Scripture as a compilation of writings ("Books") formed into an ancient literary masterpiece which deserves to be studied for its value and in ways which preserve its integrity. **We believe that the Scripture is an accurate and reliable historical, cultural and geographical record of Black people in the ancient world.** As Father Clarence Williams has aptly stated, "the Bible is a treasury of Black history."[7] It is capable of holding its own alongside other ancient historical records. When explaining the Scripture we seek to always take care to observe its teachings in their original contextual background. Thus, besides studying the Bible in a devotional manner, we plumb the depths of its message historically, culturally, theologically and spiritually. The Black presence in the Bible submits to these dimensions of Biblical exegesis.[8]

Since the Bible is very reliable historically, culturally, and geographically, the reader can depend upon it to communicate accurately what it originally intended when first written. So when the Bible identifies a person or people as "Black" (that is, African) there is no necessary reason to question what is recorded in the Scripture, as long as the Scripture is properly understood. Let us remember that Biblical information is an accurate and reliable historical, cultural and geographical record of Black peoples (and other peoples) in the ancient world, and, therefore, may be used as first-hand research resource material in its own right.[9]

2. Bible Reference Works

Bible reference works are used in a supplementary fashion to assist in the Black/African identification process and in expounding the messages contained in the related passages of Scripture. The information provided by them gives good assistance in explaining or illuminating what the Bible says. These tools are useful for understanding the historical, cultural and geographical context of the Bible. Especially useful in this area are the studies of Black historians and theologians.

The Bible reference books which we use are varied. At times we use Bible dictionaries, commentaries, atlases, encyclopedias, word studies, and others. Sometimes we use topical studies that relate to our subject.

Since many Biblical reference works are written by white or European authors, the Black Christian researcher should be careful to study these works critically, not assuming that white believers will always tell the truth. Theological and racial biases of white authors (and white-thinking authors!) sometimes hinder the discovery process of the Biblical Black presence. Black Christians who study the Bible should become accustomed to critically examining, by "looking over the shoulder" of, Bible reference tool writers to determine, as best they can, the accuracy of their information and the fairness of their opinions.

3. Extra-Biblical Writings

Third, we use extra-Biblical writings. These are books written about Black persons and places named in the Bible, but which are not written about the Bible itself. In this category we might find general encyclopedias, histories about Africa, studies about ancient Black people, cultural studies, etc.

When using Bible reference books and extra-Biblical writings we make it a priority (if at all possible) to refer first to the works of Black theologians and historians, and to give deference and more weight to their information. At times, Black writers provide information which is more fair-minded and enlightening to our subject than do European, or white American writers.

When making use of extra-Biblical sources, the student should be careful to remember that the Scripture alone is "inspired by God," and is the sole basis and standard for Christian faith and conduct. When it comes down to living the Christian faith, the Bible is the book we love and believe. Other books may help us understand the Bible and the people written about on its pages. However, no other books–whether Bible reference books or not, whether written by Christians are not, whether authored by Blacks or not–no other books take the place of the Bible in giving content to Christian beliefs and practices.

After all is said and done, in this study the Bible is our primary source for information about the Black presence within itself.

C.

Why We Speak of "Black and African"

The reader should take note that we refer to both a "Black and African" identity of the people we study. Why the distinction, one may inquire? Could we not just use the term "African" exclusively and be done with it?

1. Humanity's and Civilization's Black Roots

Popularly it would be accepted that if we are talking about "Black" people then of necessity we would be talking about a people who came from Africa. Thus we speak of African Americans, African Caribbeans, indigenous Africans (Blacks) who dwell on the continent of Africa, etc. All these groups are classified as Black people whose ancestors came from Africa and Africa itself continues to be the homeland of most Blacks in the world. Many of the people mentioned in the Bible were African and the descendants of some of them still reside there; for instance, descendants of the ancient Cushites.

In contrast, as one begins to probe the depths of the Black presence in the Bible, one discovers that from earliest times there were "Black" people living on the continent of Asia. In this vein we make reference to the people of Mesopotamian Cush ("Kish," Cf. Genesis 2:13, *AV*) and to the ancient civilization of Sumer in the land of Shinar (cf. Genesis 10:10; 11:1). According to the thinking of some scholars, the Sumerian civilization, being made predominant by Nimrod, a descendant of Cush, was prototypical in southern Asia, of Cushite origin, and had cultural affinities with Egyptian civilization.[10]

The traditional (but very outdated!) view is that the point of origination of humanity and civilization was not in the "motherland" of Africa, but in Mesopotamia in the Tigris-Euphrates Valley (if, in fact, the two places were distinct geographical territories in pre-historical times).[11] Thus, some scholars hold the position that it was from this area of Mesopotamia that Cush's descendants migrated, not from, but **into** the African mainland. Subsequently their African empire came to be known as Cush, and they inhabited, for the most part but by no means exclusively, the territory south of Egypt.[12]

Contrary to the above, the preponderance of contemporary evidence being gathered by archaeologists and ancient historians says that Africa (in Egypt's Nile Valley) was the origination of humanity and civilization. It was from here that humanity, an indigenous "Black" humanity, had its beginnings. The preponderance of archaeological and historical facts say that the roots of all people are in Africa! – **Egypt, Africa!**[13]

Whether one holds to the traditional view of a Mesopotamian origination of humanity, or to the more substantiated view of the origination of humanity in Africa, one point of harmony is certain: indigenous humanity and the originators of the civilizations in each of these areas were Black! They were Black in Egyptian Africa and they were Black in Asia's lower Mesopotamia! Either way one cuts it, the orginators of civilization were a **Black people.**[14]

The facts and arguments for Blacks being the progenitors of humanity and the originators of culture and civilization whether in consideration of the African or the Asian continent are quite convincing. Since such is the case, and realizing that the treatment of this subject will be read by persons holding either view, we are pressed to use terminology in this study which identifies both "African" people as well as other "Black" people whom some scholars regard as not having originated in Africa. We believe this procedure does no violence to our main objective, which is to identify the specific persons and nations in the Bible whom we regard as being Black and/or African.

2. Indigenous Black Africans

There is another reason we refer to "Black" people in this study, rather than refer exclusively to African people. This is because when we speak of "African" in this study we are speaking of an indigenous **Black** people.   Not all people who lived in Africa (or who live there now!) were Black or regarded as such by students of history.   Over the centuries there were migrations into Africa by other people who were in fact and/or who were deemed "non-Black."[15]

We strive to make a clear point: when we reference African people we mean **Black** African people.   Granted there are arguments as to what constitutes "Blackness," yet in this study we are highlighting whatever Blackness is discernible and understandable in Biblical people.   The primary focus and priority of this study is concerned with Black African people wherever found in the Biblical world.   We then address its implications as they impact other people of "color" mentioned in the Scripture, especially in their associations with Black/African people.   This study is in the very least concerned with identifying any people considered (most often in perpetuation of racism with disregard for the truth) "white" Africans.[16]   Our concern is for identifying Biblical **Black** Africans.

The following words by Dr. Charles B. Copher serve to set the context for the preceding point:

> The more or less biblically based view that regarded the black man as an inhabitant of the biblical world may be titled the Old Hamite Hypothesis...Then, around 1800, a new stream came to the surface. This latter, which may be called the New Hamite Hypothesis, eliminates the black man, or rather the so-called Negro, from the biblical world. Those black peoples whom it retains are given the title Caucasoid Blacks who instead of being regarded as Negroes are viewed as being white.[17] [The] new Hamite hypothesis or view... dissociated the so-called Negroes from the Hamites, removes color from the criteria for determining racial identity, and regards black non-Negroids to be white – Caucasoid or Europid Blacks. It is this view or hypothesis which came to characterize the so-called sciences of anthropology, ethnology, and kindred studies, but also critical historical-literacy Biblical studies. And just as anthropology and ethnology removed Negroes from the Biblical world so did critical study of the Bible remove Negroes from the Bible and Biblical history – except for an occasional Negro individual who

could only have been a slave. Thus today in critical Biblical studies, as in anthropology and ethnology, the ancient Egyptians, Cushites, in fact all the Biblical Hamites, were white; so-called Negroes did not figure at all in Biblical history, and there could not have been interaction between Blacks and Jews if by Blacks is meant so-called Negroes.[18]

3. "Black": An Ancient Ethnological Self-Definition

A third reason why we refer to identifying "Black and African" people in this study is because ancient Blacks described themselves, and the people of their lands, by their color, their dark **Black** color. This was true of the ancient peoples of Cush, Egypt and Sumer.[19] This ancient means of Black self-identification occurred long before the modern anthropological and ethnological studies divided up humanity (according to one classification) into "races" called "black," "brown," "yellow," "red," and "white"![20]

The use of "Black" as an ethnological self-identification by far antedates the use of "African," a term of relatively recent usage.[21] This usage of "Black" as an ethnological self-identification is also present within the Biblical data, and it actually does a great service in facilitating the process of discovery and identification of Black persons and nations mentioned in the Scripture. At times, therefore, our use of the term "Black" may be more accurate and get at the heart of the matter than the use of the term "African." Parenthetically, in the U.S. Census survey, an American Black should have taken care to identify himself as "Black," (or "Negro"), the legal/technical categories for our race. Whenever "Other race" was checked and "African-American" written, it served only to dilute the representation of American Blacks as a whole.

4. Global Geopolitics

Nevertheless, we choose not to use the term "Black" exclusively. Due to the need for Black cultural and national identity and unity, and to the situation of global geopolitics, both "Black" and "African" are needed as racial/ethnic identifiers to facilitate the liberation and well-being of Black/African people the world around, and particularly of African Blacks in America. This is our fourth and final reason for using "Black and African."

To summarize, the use of "Black and African" together in this study 1) helps to draw the attention of those holding either view of humanity's and civilization's origin (Asia's Mesopotamia or Africa's Egypt) to its Black roots; 2) focuses the primary scope of this subject as dealing with **Black** African people; 3) highlights the ancient ethnological self-definition of Black peoples who used their dark skin color as a main criterion in identifying and projecting who they were: **Black**; and 4) facilitates the liberation and well-being of Black African-Americans engaged in the global struggle for Black people's survival.

D.

The Definition of Blackness Used in the Study

The forementioned discussion and position set the stage for defining what we mean by "Black." What is our understanding of "Blackness" when it is said that there is a "Black" presence in the Scripture? Contrary to the popular opinions of many who think the Bible is the "white man's book," most personages mentioned in the Scripture were "people of color." Yet, this study is concerned with a particular people of color–Black people.

When we affirm that there is a Black presence in the Bible, we are affirming a definition of Blackness which includes the following. **First**, actual "black" skin color;[22] **second**, so-called "Negroid" characteristics; and **third**, traceable Black or African ancestry ("Black blood"). If a Biblical person is identified as Black, he/she will possess these characteristics. To cite Dr. Charles B. Copher:

> When I speak of Black peoples and personalities in the Bible, by Black I mean three things. First of all I mean to define Black literally, so one is literally Black. Secondly, I define Black to mean what we mean sociologically here in America. That a person having any discernible trace of African, Negroid blood, is Black. And then, thirdly, by Black I mean, Black from an anthropological perspective. One is negroid, having what the anthropologists regard as negroid features, such as black color, thick lips, kinky hair, and so on. So when I speak of Black I am meaning those three things all at one and the same time.[23]

1. Actual "Black" Skin Color

First, concerning actual "black" color. There were Black people in the Biblical world who were ethnologically identified (both by themselves and their neighbors) in terms of their color. The very names of these persons and nations mean "Black" (e.g., Cush,

Genesis 10:6), or these persons and nations are spoken of with the qualifying adjective signifying Black color (e.g., Simeon called "Niger," that is "Black," Acts 13:1).[24]

2. So-called "Negroid" Characteristics

Second, concerning so-called "Negroid" characteristics. When we refer to "Black" under this dimension of ethnicity, our concentration in this study is on Biblical people with primarily African ancestral origins–native or indigenous African roots. Such aboriginal African people are the essential measure of what it means to be "Negroid." This identification is anthropological and ethnological in nature, and includes such characteristics as black color, hair-type, and skeletal structure, particularly as related to the cranial.[25]

It is interesting to note that the criteria or basis for measuring this anthropological/ethnological identification of what is "Negroid" (as over against what is "Caucasoid") was developed by white men.[26] Of course, they made their criteria to the advantage of themselves and their people. Yet, they made it and consequently are having to face living with its repercussions–often repercussions which are devastating to the white psyche. For when archaeologists dig up human bones and measure them, they are discovering overwhelmingly that the oldest known human remains are "Negroid", not "Caucasoid."

3. Ancestral "Black Blood"

Third, concerning traceable Black or African ancestry, "Black blood." Biblical Black persons and nations may be identified through their roots, their ancestry. It is commonly accepted that, for the most part, Black peoples Biblically defined are descendants of Ham, one of the sons of Noah. Thus they are known as "Hamitic" people. So Biblical people possessing "Black blood," are descendants of Black and/or indigenous African people, especially (though not exclusively) of Hamitic people.   We will present more on this later.

Suffice it now to say that Biblical genealogical tables, "family trees," become crucial in the Black identification process.   For example, studying the family lineage of the tribe of Joseph ("Ephraim and Manasseh"),[27] or studying the genealogy of David[28] through which the Messiah came, proves most enlightening and yields substantial rewards in the specific identification process.

Notice that this "Black blood" category relates to the popular American definition of what constitutes a Black person.   This definition teaches that a person who has any traces of "Black blood" running through his veins (from his lineal ancestral forebears) is legally and nationally,[29] racially, and ethnically classified as a Black American (or African American).   This definition is applicable despite the "lightness" of a Black person's skin color, or the apparent number of "Caucasoid" traits he/she possesses.[30]

The fact must be kept in mind that the vast majority of white Americans consider Black any person who possesses any, however small, amount of "Black blood."[31]   Being "fair" to this white American definition, we apply the same criterion of who is Black to Biblical persons and nations. White people, including those who are Christian, cannot have their cake and eat it too!

If the legal and popularly held criteria of Blackness is good enough (!) for African Americans, it is also a good enough criteria to apply as a rule of exegesis[32] to the numerous people mentioned in the Scripture.   One result of this consistent application is that when the "Black blood" definition of Black peoples is applied to the ethnological identification of Biblical personages, this definition substantially disarms many white scholars and people who erroneously seek to whitenize numerous Black and African people of the Bible world, particularly the ancient Egyptians.[33]

E.

The Bible's Explicit, Implicit and Presumed

Black Presence

1. The Explicit Black Presence

There is both an **implicit**, an **explicit**, as well as a **presumed** Black presence in the Bible. Most students can readily grasp the explicit presence of Blacks in the Scripture. They are quick to name specific persons such as Simon of Cyrene, the crossbearer for Jesus (Mark 15:21); the Ethiopian eunuch who was converted through the witness of Philip (Acts 8:26-40); the Cushite woman whom Moses married (Numbers 12:1ff); the Queen of Sheba who visited King Solomon, (1 Kings 10:1-13), and others. These students may also identify certain peoples and nations who are Black, referring to those such as the ancient Egyptians (e.g., Genesis 12:12, 14; Exodus 1:13, 19; Leviticus 24:10); the Cushites (or "Ethiopians," e.g., 2 Chronicles 12:3, Jeremiah 46:9) or even to the Midianites (e.g., Genesis 37:28, 36; Numbers 10:29; 25:6; Judges 6-7) and the Hittites (e.g., Genesis 15:20; 23:10; Exodus 3:8; Joshua 1:4; 1 Kings 10:29). There is clear Scriptural data which demonstrates the Blackness of all these persons and nations.

2. The Implicit Black Presence

However, and perhaps more important, there is also an implicit Black presence in the Bible which students need to discover and understand. That is, we need to affirm the identity of a people whose social milieu is composed to some degree of Blackness and/or Africanness, but whose individual personages escape precise Black identification. Their Blackness is not ascertainable, it is implied rather than expressly stated. This area of study can be most enlightening and fascinating.

For instance, how would the reader's perception of the

Abrahamic Hebrew community's ethnic make-up be affected by a factual understanding demonstrating to him that the territory in Mesopotamia from which Abraham migrated, Ur of the Chaldees (Genesis 11:28, 31; 15:7; Nehemiah 9:7), was inhabited by a Black people?[34] Or, how does it challenge our thinking to understand that the "mixed multitude" (Exodus 12:37-38) who left Egypt with the Children of Israel included many native Egyptians whose numbers probably far surpassed the population who were descendants from Jacob's twelve sons?[35] Does it make any difference that scholars can verify that at certain times the inhabitants of the Mediterranean islands of Crete[36] and Cyprus[37] contained Black peoples among their populations?[38]

The implicit Black presence in the Bible can be traced also along other lines throughout Biblical history. To mention several other areas of investigation, we can study 1) the Black identification of peoples and nations all over the world of the Bible;[39] 2) the Egyptian names of persons in Moses' family;[40] 3) the intermixture of the Canaanites, an explicitly Hamitic Black people, with the Israelite population;[41] and 4) the impacting of Christ's ancestral lineal genealogy with persons known to be Black.[42]

These implicit lines of thought demonstrating the Black presence in the Scriptures set a good context for understanding and better appreciating the explicit Biblical references to Black persons and nations. **Thanks to the implicit Black presence in the Bible, we have good grounds for believing that many of the numerous and diverse names of persons mentioned in Scripture reference Black people, but yet we have no good way of explicitly identifying them as such.**

3. The Presumed Black Presence

The world of the Bible was a world composed of different peoples. That world of different peoples served as the cultural and social background to Biblical history. This world of different peoples included mostly people of color and an overwhelming majority of Black peoples. Thus, a major assumption in this investigation is that there was indeed a Black presence in the world which gave us the Bible.[43]

That is, at the time when the events of Scripture took place, and over the period of time when the books of the Bible were first written, there were Black peoples inhabiting the then known world. Many of these Black peoples had direct dealings with the covenant people of the Bible. Consequently, many of these Black persons and nations were plainly identified and others were referred to indirectly in the Bible.[44] This identification was natural, for these were the same Black people inhabiting the then known world. **Therefore, any explanations of Scripture in their historical and cultural contexts ought as a matter of sound exegetical course make reference to these Black persons and nations. The fruits of any serious Biblical study must of necessity include the presence of Black people.[45]**

As a further matter of consideration, it is the author's position that, especially in regards to the Old Testament, the student can with good conscience based on solid evidence **presume the Blackness** of any given Biblical personality unless there is concrete evidence to the contrary. This is the distinct impression one receives having evaluated the information about the world of the Bible. The Blackness of the Biblical world was pervasive.[46]

F.

The Transformation of Black Identity

As may have already been ascertained, the author's pursuit of this subject is at heart more than for the purpose of intellectual stimulation. Since all Scripture is inspired by God,[47] then that which the Bible records about Black people is also inspired—and profitable! **Hopefully, the Black readers of this sacred study will undergo such a radical transformation of their Black identity from the spiritual ground of its roots in God, that they will rise up for the cause of the liberation of themselves and for the redemption of the world by God through Christ Jesus the Lord. All to the glory of God.**

SECTION II

The Process of Identification

A. Ways for Identifying Black People in the Bible

B. From the Obvious to the More Difficult

C Identifying Individual Persons and Nations

D. Data & Freqency of Several Biblical Names

Referencing Black People

A.

Ways for Identifying Black People in the Bible

The process used in identifying the Black presence in the Bible is most important. We chose to use sound methods of identifying and to highlight Black Biblical persons and nations whose Blackness can later be verified and substantiated by the reader. Therefore, when we assert that a particular individual or nation is Black, we will then proceed to give the basis and reasoning for such an identification.

The reader will soon discover that Black people mentioned in the Scripture may be identified 1) through names and adjectives; 2) through their ancestors, family trees; 3) through extra-Biblical information gained from other areas of study including archaeology, anthropology, culture, etc.; and 4) through chronological correlation with the Black ethnic make-up of peoples in the Biblical world.[48]

1. Names / Adjectives

One of the easiest ways to identify Black people in the Bible is through the use of names.[49] There are three kinds of names which may be used to help identify Black people in the Bible: personal names, people names, and place names.

Names in the Bible are usually impregnated with much meaning. The meaning of some of these names make reference to a person's or nation's racial/ethnic origin. This is particularly so in the case of the personal name of an individual. An example of an identifying Black personal name is "Kedar" ("very Black"),[50] or "Phinehas" ("the Negro," or "the Nubian");[51] an example of a people or national name is "Cush" ("Black");[52] and an example of a place name is "Tahpanhes" (Jeremiah 43:7; "Palace of the Negro")[53] or "Ham," indicating "hot," "heat," "Black."[54]

Closely associated with the use of personal names are qualifying adjectives. For example, Moses' Black wife is twice called a

"Cushite woman" (Numbers 12:1), and Simeon the prophet, a leading member of the Church at Antioch is nicknamed "Niger" meaning "dark-complexioned" (Acts 13:1).[55]

A variety of Biblical names can be used to identify Black people. Some of these names are prominent in the Scripture. If someone uses a concordance to begin searching for terms useful for identifying Black people, he or she will not find certain popular terms. For instance, in the Bible the researcher will not find "Colored," "Negro," "African," "Afro-American," or "African-American." None of these popular names referencing Black people are found in Bible concordances because these terms are not used in Bible times or Biblical writings.

There are some names identifying Blacks/Africans which will, however, be uncovered by use of a concordance. "Black" will be found numerous times. But it will only be cited twice in one passage of Scripture with respect to a person's racial/ethnic identity. This reference is Song of Solomon 1:5, 6. There the Shulamite of King Solomon's love says "I am **black**, and beautiful, O daughters of Jerusalem, like the tents of Kedar, like the curtains of Solomon. Do not look at me because I am **blackened**, because the sun has looked upon me."[56]

2. Ancestors / Family Trees

A second useful way for identifying Black people in the Bible is through their ancestors. This is through the area of kindred blood relation/association. We call this the "family tree." Understanding this process is simple. If an individual's great-grandmother, for example, was African, so is the individual. For instance, Zephaniah the prophet's father was named "Cushi" (Zephaniah 1:1). Thus, the prophet Zephaniah is classified as Black by virtue of his natural father. So, if Black is the root, so is the fruit![57]

There are a number of Black/African family trees in Scripture. Studying them is most rewarding and enlightening. One can study the family trees of Ham's four sons: "Cush," "Egypt," "Put," and "Canaan" (Genesis 10:6-20). Then one can study the family trees of Joseph through his sons Ephraim and Manasseh (Numbers

26:28-37); of King Hezekiah, the great-grandfather of Cushi, Zephaniah's father (Zephaniah 1:1; 2 Kings 18:1; 20:21; 21:1); of Judah through Tamar (1 Chronicles 2:3, 4-5ff.); of David through Solomon (2 Samuel 12:24; 2 Chronicles 3:5; 1 Kings 14:21, 31), etc.

3. Extra-Biblical Information

A third avenue for identifying Black people in the Bible is through **extra-Biblical information** gained by use of reference books, whether written about the Bible or not. These reference works may in nature be archaeological, historical, geographical, ethnological, cultural, linguistic, anthropological or the like. This way for identifying Biblical Blacks is established first outside the Scripture. This content is then used to better understand the Biblical reference. This process can be most rewarding. It works in this fashion.

Suppose we discover a Biblical name which cannot be traced in the Black family tree back to a known Black and/or African ancestor. We could then search other reference books and materials to determine the anthropological and/or ethnological identification of these people. In some cases, our search will yield the finding that a given people were indeed a Black or African people. Such an identification would be valuable even though the process of verification was not based in the Scripture.

As a case in point of the above means for identifying Biblical Blacks we refer to the ancient people known as "Elam" mentioned in Genesis 10:22. **First,** we find no clues to their ethnic identification from their name, whose meaning is uncertain, and perhaps means "high land."[58] **Second,** according to Genesis chapter 10, the ancestry of Elam does not trace back to Ham, the commonly accepted father of African peoples. Indeed, Elam is listed as a descendant of Shem (Genesis 10:22). **Third,** however, when we look to other sources of information seeking to gain information about Elam, we discover that ancient Elam contained a predominant Black presence from its roots![59] Moreover, **fourth,** a fringe benefit to this discovery establishes an explicit Black line within the family tree of Shem![60]

4. Chronological Correlation

The names and adjectives mentioned above cannot be the sole basis for establishing the Black/African identity of Biblical people. For names reflect not only people, but also places. And specific geographical areas have over different time-periods often been inhabited by people of a different ethnic or national origin than a geographical territory's indigenous population. Hence, the dating of Biblical events and persons, and tracing the movements of people, which in other theological discussions may be inconsequential, may prove critical to certain dimensions of this type of discussion.

However, once the Blackness of a given people, in a specific land, during a delineated time-period has been established, then any Biblical references to these people by their contemporaries can be used as an affirmation of a person's or people's Blackness. An example of such usage can be found in the Book of Zephaniah. There the prophet speaks of the people called the "Cushites," as well as of "the rivers of Cush" (2:12; 3:10, *NIV*). Zephaniah was well aware of these Black people. The Cushites were well-known at the time in history when Zephaniah wrote the words of his prophecy (in the 7th century B.C.). Zephaniah was also well aware of how his ethnology would be understood when he referred to himself as "the son of Cushi" (1:1).[61]

B.

From the Obvious to the More Difficult

As the researcher begins his study, he would do well to initially focus his concentration on explicit Biblical persons and nations about whom there is little debate concerning their Black identification. He should study Biblical personages who are obviously Black. These are persons and nations who are identified as Black by themselves, and by other Biblical people and writers. Thus, they are clearly identified by the people who lived among them, who distinctly noted them for their evident degree of Blackness, and/or compared-contrasted these people to themselves.

Proceeding through the study, the researcher should find himself/ herself moving into those areas where simple references will establish the Blackness of a given person or nation. Ultimately, the student will approach the more difficult tasks where the careful weighing of facts and the considered judgment of the author weighs heavily in the identification procedure.

C.

Identifying Individual Persons and Nations

Both Black **persons** as well as **nations** are subjects included in the scope of this study. Individual personalities are important. After all, God created individual personalities, both male and female, in His image and after His likeness. Thus, each Black person mentioned in Scripture has value and is of value for us in our study. There is much to be learned from the study and exemplary models of individual Black men and women, and, perhaps, of boys and girls, in the Scripture.

Yet, we need to also gain a perspective on the broader picture wherein Biblical Black individuals carried on their lives. We must come to see the Black individuals of Scripture as their roles are unfolded within their Black nations. As Biblical students we must endeavor to discover and understand the gifts, cultures, interactions, and destinies of Black nations as they moved throughout the Biblical world. Consequently, the explanation of information about Black nations is an essential part of this Biblical study.

In dealing with what qualifies a group of people being constituted and classified as a "nation," we work with two concepts. There is one concept of "nation" which references the whole population of a territory, with emphasis on the political and social dimensions of a people's experience. They are sufficiently conscious of their unity to seek or to possess their own unique government. Such a group lives under an organized government, occupies a fixed area, and deals as a unit with other similar groups. They have strong systemic ties.

A second concept of "nation" references a group of people with common blood ties and close family connections especially on the father's side. Kinship bonds are at the fore. They are not a regimented organization. They may be regarded as a "clan," "extended family," or, more affectively, as a "people," for they are of the same ethnic family and speak the same language. They have common interests and a unified culture. Their emotional ties are strong.[62]

There are various groups of Black people mentioned within the Scripture who possess either of the "nation" characteristics mentioned above. Some of these Black groups were highly politically and socially organized, for example the Egyptians or the Assyrians. Others were held together more by blood ties and common interests than anything else, for example the Midianites or the Kedarites. Most, if not all, may be classified as nations. There is much to be learned from both types of nations in our study of the Bible's Black presence. The lessons we learn can contribute substantively to the development of nationhood among Black Africans in America.

D.

Data & Frequency of Several

Biblical Names Referencing Black People

According to the following data, the reader may gain a general overview of several names used in the Bible referencing Black people.[63] The first part provides information about **Ham**, the father of African peoples, and his sons: **Cush**, **Egypt**,[64] **Put**, and **Canaan**. In the second part we are provided with information about several Black people and nations chosen at random.[65] The third part gives names of people associated with the lineage of Cush according to Genesis 10:7-8.[66]

Name	Number of Occurrences
Ham	17
Cush	9
Cushan	1
Cushan-Rishathaim	4
Cushi	2
Cushite	10
Ethiopia	19
Ethiopian	7
Ethiopians	12
Egypt	617
Egypt's	3
Egyptian	24
Egyptian's	3
Egyptians	103
Put	8
Canaan	87
Canaanite	11
Canaanites	61
Canaanitess	1
Canaanitish	1

Persons	Number of Occurrences[67]
Melchizedek Genesis 14:18; Psalm 110:4; Hebrews 5:6, 10; 6:20; 7:1, 10, 11, 15, 17	10
Ephron the Hittite Genesis 23:8, 10, 13, 14, 16, 17; 25:9; 49:29, 30; 50:13	12
Hagar the Egyptian Genesis 16:1, 3, 4, 8, 15, 16; 21:9, 14, 17; 25:12; Galatians 4:24, 25	14
Rahab the Harlot Joshua 2:1, 3; 6:17, 23, 25; Matthew 1:5; Hebrews 11:31; James 2:25	8
Queen of Sheba 1 Kings 10:1, 4, 10, 13; 2 Chronicles 9:1, 3, 9, 12; Matthew 12:42; Luke 11:31	10
Ebedmelech the Ethiopian Jeremiah 38:7, 8, 10, 11, 12; 39:16	6
Pharaoh Tirhakah 2 Kings 19:9; Isaiah 37:9	2

Nations	Number of Occurrences
Midian	51
Midianite	5
Midianites	12
Kedar	12
Elam	17
Elamites	2
Hittite	26
Hittites	35

Cush Descendant	Number of Occurrences
Seba	4
Havilah	7
Sabta(h)	2
Raama(h)	5
Sheba	17
Dedan	8
Sabteca	2
Nimrod	4
Asshur	5

SECTION III

Focusing Our Study

A. The Importance of the Study,

   Especially for Black People

B. Identifying Blackness Popularly

A.

The Importance of the Study,

Especially for Black People

The Bible records the story of God's unfolding drama of redemption. God's Redeemer is the Lord Jesus Christ, the Son of God, the Son of Man.[68]   Jesus' supreme act of redemption took place on a hill outside the city of Jerusalem called Calvary. There Jesus was criminally crucified on a cross for all humanity.[69] He died for our sin and in our place. He died in order to bring humanity back into a right relationship with God our Creator.[70]

Since the Bible discloses God's message of redemption, it is obviously concerned with people–all people. For all people from every race and ethnic group of humanity need to be redeemed and thus need to hear and understand God's Word of redemption as it is focused in Jesus. For all people have sinned and have fallen short of God's glory. Implicitly or explicitly it is revealed in the Bible that every group of people are included in God's redemption circle. So from its beginning to its end the Bible provides information about numerous nations, tribes, peoples, and tongues and about God's dealings with them.[71]

Of the many peoples who are mentioned and highlighted in the Scripture are Black peoples – African peoples. They too are the objects of God's redeeming grace. They too are the vessels whom God uses to spread His message of redemption to the world.

The student who searches the Scripture will find that explicit Black people were genuine and pertinent members of the Biblical community of faith. In fact, the Old Testament community of faith was Black in its roots! Black people lived under both the Old Covenant and the New Covenant. Their presence and importance were not inflated, but neither were they negated. God had (and has) His hand upon these African people–people of deep dark color.

It is important especially for Black American people to appreciate the Black presence in the Scripture. It is important historically, because the Bible is history. It is recorded history from God's perspective. And it is reliable history. Black people need to understand all Black history, including that which is revealed in the Bible. If we are ignorant of our history and its heritage we will walk blindly into our future. And without keeping in our minds and hearts the spiritual and eternal dimensions of our history, our future forebodes a hopelessness which many of us would rather not face.

From a Christian viewpoint it is important for Black people to understand their Biblical history. Understanding the Black presence within the Bible nurtures among Black people an affection for the Scripture and the things of the Lord. Far too many of our people reject the Bible because they don't understand that it speaks responsibly about them and to their experience. God is concerned about Black people. Furthermore, enough information pertaining to Black people and their experience is written in His Word to convince the honest searcher for truth that God is indeed concerned for the well-being, salvation and liberation of Black peoples throughout the world.

The road to spiritual maturity is through Christian education based on the whole of Scripture. "All Scripture is inspired by God" and has a part to play in the wholistic Christian development of each believer (2 Timothy 3:16-17). Since this is so, why do Black Christians, if they want to be made whole, neglect those things which God has graciously said about Black people in His Word? The Lord had to say what He has said about Black people for some reason, some good reason.

It is time for Black Christians to read, study and draw lessons for themselves from those things which God has ordained to be written about Black people in His Word. The Black presence is not the entire focus of the Bible, but neither should its contribution be neglected or despised. Black people must learn to appreciate those words of God which are specifically addressed to them and about them as a people.

B.

Identifying Blackness Popularly

Popularly, "Blackness" can be identified in four ways. To a certain degree, these views may relate to identifying Black people in the Bible. These four integrated perspectives can provide an insight into identifying Biblical Black people and an avenue for communicating to the popular mind those persons and nations so identified.

1. Black people are identifiable by natural characteristics, particularly by the color of their skin. In the Bible, Jeremiah asked of Black people, "Can the Ethiopian change his skin...?" (13:23).

We identify those who are Black as those who are naturally assumed as such. They are basically an African people. Most are of a dark hue in color, and "Negroid" in physical characteristic to a far greater degree than other peoples. In the Scripture, no special attention is drawn to their identity. They are named and identified just as any other Biblical character, or just named period. They are merely accepted at "face" value, by their dark color – the initially impressionable criterion for identifying Black people especially. What is seen is who they are.

2. Black people are identifiable by their negation by others. In the Bible, Aaron and Miriam sought to place themselves a class above Moses' Black wife, for they "spoke against Moses because of the Cushite woman whom he had married, for he had married a Cushite woman" (Numbers 12:1). This controversy revealed a political power grab by Aaron and Miriam challenging Moses' headship of the liberated community of Israel (Cf. Numbers 12:2-8ff.).

Popularly we identify those who are Black as those African people who are negated. For the most part, this definition is imposed upon Black people by outsiders, particularly by the despicable term "nigger" used by whites of Blacks, as well as by

Blacks in reference to themselves. This negation is rooted in racism and perpetuated through social oppression.

When a certain person is identifiable as coming from a race or ethnic group different from the white majority-dominant group, this person is stigmatized and treated with contempt by the group in power. These, indeed, are the "niggers" of the society. Ofttimes those who are oppressed internalize how the oppressor feels about them and perpetuate this psycho-social violence on themselves and on their own people. There are many Blacks who have internalized and reinforce in various ways this negative definition of Blackness. Thus "nigger" is at times a racial distinction and at other times a class distinction, dependent upon who uses the term for what purpose.[72]

3. Black people are identifiable by their own self-affirmation, particularly in reference to their value and beauty. In the Bible, the Shulamite of Solomon's Song proclaimed of her Black being, "I am black and beautiful" (1:5).[73]

We identify those who are Black as those who accept and identify themselves as such. Theirs is a self-imposed positive definition. Aesthetically, it expresses a high value which Black persons place upon their own being, culture and experience. Being positive, this definition reflects more than a reactive response to racism. It is a pro-active response based on standards reflecting noble human and personhood values.

4. Black people are identifiable by the choice of their association, particularly under oppressive circumstances. In the Bible, Moses chose "rather to share ill-treatment with the people of God," (Hebrews 11:25). In doing so, Moses identified with his own Black people who were regarded as the covenant people of God and whose ranks included many native Egyptians.

We identify those who are Black as those who choose to operate in Black community. So to speak, they have put their "name on the roll" of Black nationhood. They have decided to identify with and operate concertedly with their people. Some of them, for instance, could choose to identify with the other side of their mixed-parentage, but go the other way. Some of them could "pass," but they choose not to. Some of them could hold to limited definitions of Blackness and by doing so individualistically function in society, but they don't. Like Moses, they choose to operate in Black community.[74]

SECTION IV

The Table of Nations and the
Hamitic Black/African Genealogical Line
Genesis 10:1-32

A. Introduction to Genesis 10

B. Background to Genesis 10

C. Understanding the Table's Structure

A.

Introduction to Genesis 10

Genesis chapter 10 is a passage of Scripture which is foundational to the study of the Black presence in the Bible. Studying this passage will probably do more to assist the reader in understanding the roots and relationships of Biblical Blacks than perhaps any other passage of Scripture. Much of what is taught about the Bible's Black presence, whether dealing with individuals or nations, leads us back in one way or another to *Genesis 10*.

The sections below are from the complementary volume to this study. It is entitled **The Black Presence in the Bible and The Table of Nations – Genesis 10:1-32: with emphasis on the Hamitic Genealogical Line from a Black Perspective.** The reader is referred to that volume for an in-depth analysis and documentation of information summarized here.

The Text of Genesis 10 *(RSV)*

Following is a printing of Genesis 10:1-32 from the *Revised Standard Version*. Its major divisions are indicated by paragraphs.

{1} These are the generations of the sons of Noah, Shem, Ham, and Japheth; sons were born to them after the flood.

{2} The sons of Japheth: Gomer, Magog, Madai, Javan, Tubal, Meshech, and Tiras. {3} The sons of Gomer: Ashkenaz, Riphath, and Togarmah. {4} The sons of Javan: Elishah, Tarshish, Kittim, and Dodanim. {5} From these the coastland peoples spread. These are the sons of Japheth in their lands, each with his own language, by their families, in their nations.

{6} The sons of Ham: Cush, Egypt, Put, and Canaan. {7} The sons of Cush: Seba, Havilah, Sabtah, Raamah, and Sabteca. The sons of Raamah: Sheba and Dedan. {8} Cush became the father of Nimrod; he was the first on earth to be a mighty man. {9} He was a mighty hunter before the LORD; therefore it is said, "Like Nimrod a mighty hunter before the LORD." {10} The beginning of his kingdom was Babel, Erech, and Accad, all of them in the land of Shinar. {11} From that land he went into Assyria, and built Nineveh, Rehoboth-Ir, Calah, and {12} Resen between Nineveh and Calah; that is the great city. {13} Egypt became the father of Ludim, Anamim, Lehabim, Naphtuhim, {14} Pathrusim, Casluhim (whence came the Philistines), and Caphtorim. {15} Canaan became the father of Sidon his first-born, and Heth, {16} and the Jebusites, the Amorites, the Girgashites, {17} the Hivites, the Arkites, the Sinites, {18} the Arvadites, the Zemarites, and the Hamathites. Afterward the families of the Canaanites spread abroad. {19} And the territory of the Canaanites extended from Sidon, in the direction of Gerar, as far as Gaza, and in the direction of Sodom, Gomorrah, Admah, and Zeboiim, as far as Lasha. {20} These are the sons of Ham, by their families, their languages, their lands, and their nations.

{21} To Shem also, the father of all the children of Eber, the elder brother of Japheth, children were born. {22} The sons of Shem: Elam, Asshur, Arpachshad, Lud, and Aram. {23} The sons of Aram: Uz, Hul, Gether, and Mash. {24} Arpachshad became the father of Shelah; and Shelah became the father of Eber. {25} To Eber were born two sons: the name of the one was Peleg, for in his days the earth was divided, and his brother's name was Joktan. {26} Joktan became the father of Almodad, Sheleph, Hazarmaveth, Jerah, {27} Hadoram, Uzal, Diklah, {28} Obal, Abimael, Sheba, {29} Ophir, Havilah, and Jobab; all these were the sons of Joktan. {30} The territory in which they lived extended from Mesha in the direction of Sephar to the hill country of the east. {31} These are the sons of Shem, by their families, their languages, their lands, and their nations.

{32} These are the families of the sons of Noah, according to their genealogies, in their nations; and from these the nations spread abroad on the earth after the flood.

A broad outline of Genesis 10:1-32.

```
I.      Heading (1)
II.     Japheth's Descendants (2-5)
III.    Ham's Descendants (6-20)
IV.     Shem's Descendants (21-31)
V.      Summary Inscription (32)
```

B.

Background to Genesis 10

1. Its Names – A Key to Humanity's Identity

Genesis 10 is a look at ancient humanity. The look is made through numerous names, over 70. These names are connected one to the other and thus provide an indication of the interrelationships of ancient peoples. Names are useful for two main purposes. Basically, a name is a handle of **identification**. It is the means by which we specify and recognize people. In addition, a name may also serve to express the **identity** of a person or people. It is often through names that we came to discover and appreciate who a person or people actually is. Though many of the names in *Genesis 10* do not have any immediate or obvious reference point for many people, a study of these names will yield the fruit of establishing the identity of the ancient persons and people behind these names. The identity of peoples composing Black humanity waits to be unlocked in many of the names found in *Genesis 10*.

2. A Unique Document

Genesis 10 is a unique passage of Scripture, being a document in its own right, and a one-of-a-kind historical writing. This ancient historiographic literary piece provides basic information about the origin and classification of especially peoples and nations in the ancient world. There is no other ancient document either within or outside the Bible which comes close to providing the detailed information provided in *Genesis 10*. Historical researchers have searched in vain for a document which can match its contents.

That *Genesis 10* may serve as a document in its own right can be seen by observing its place among the ten family histories which compose the entire book of Genesis.

Ten Histories

History 1: Genesis 1:1–4:26. The generations of the heavens
          and the earth
History 2: Genesis 5:1–6:8. The generations of Adam
History 3: Genesis 6:9–9:29. The generations of Noah
History 4: Genesis 10:1–11:9. The generations of Noah's sons
History 5: Genesis 11:10–26. The generations of Shem
History 6: Genesis 11:27–25:11. The generations of Terah
History 7: Genesis 25:12–18. The generations of Ishmael
History 8: Genesis 25:19–35:29. The generations of Isaac
History 9: Genesis 36:1–37:1. The generations of Esau
History 10: Genesis 37:2–50:26. The generations of Jacob[75]

Of the ten histories, *Genesis 10* would fall within history 4, the generations of Noah's sons, which also includes the event that occurred at Babel (Genesis 10:1-11:9).

3. Its Value

The uniqueness of *Genesis 10* points directly to its worth. Much of the value and importance of this passage of Scriptures lies in the fact that through it we can identify the origins of many of the peoples living today. That is, most of the nations we see in the world today can usually be traced back to a person or people whose name is provided in *Genesis 10*. It is possible for many Black peoples the world over to trace their roots back to an ancient ancestor in this passage. *Genesis 10* is in some measure a veritable "African Family Tree." However, in addition to providing us with ancestral links, this unique passage also provides us with other geographical and political information which serves only to embellish our important Black genealogical roots.

4. A "Genealogical Table"

Genesis 10 is more than a "genealogy" as popularly understood. Its contents cannot be limited to providing "a record of a continuous unbroken line of descent of one's physical ancestry." Biblical genealogies vary. They may be no more than a simple listing of names. On the other hand, they may be an extended historical record based on a framework of names. *Genesis 10* is neither. Its contents fit the kind of Biblical genealogy which links names with a set formula while providing additional information inserted selectively. At points, *Genesis 10* contains gaps called "telescoping." At times it does not give full treatment equally to all descendants.

For this reason, it is good to view *Genesis 10* as a "Table of Nations," the traditional name assigned to it by Biblical scholars. Sometimes its names are simply a bare listing of names as one would find in a "table." In all actuality, *Genesis 10* is a "Genealogical

Table," for it shares characteristics of each. We will usually refer to it as the "Table of Nations," or just as the "Table."

5. Noah's Descendants

The Table provides us with information about the descendants of Noah and his three sons, Shem, Ham, and Japheth. It gives us vital information about the repopulation of the earth by Noah's sons following the Flood (Genesis 9:1, 19; 10:1, 32). In Biblical usage, the descendants of Shem are called "Semites," (or "Semitic;" "Shemite" or "Shemitic), of Ham are called "Hamites" (or "Hamitic"), and of Japheth are called "Japhethites" (or Japhetic). (The reader should be aware that there is also a linguistic usage of "Semitic" and "Hamitic." Refer to section "Ham and Hamitic Descendants: B. 'Understanding Hamitic'.")

Although the Scripture (Genesis 9:19) is clear to this reader, stating that Noah's three sons repopulated the entire earth following the Flood in which everyone else had been destroyed (according to 1 Peter 3:20), the Table of Nations does not claim to name all the descendants of Noah's sons. It does not cite all the people of the earth in its listing. For instance, the Chinese are not mentioned by name, neither are the Blacks who were in America B.C.[76]

According to the genealogical passages of Genesis 5:32 and 1 Chronicles 1:4, and other verses, the order of Noah's sons is "Shem, Ham, and Japheth." Ham was the second born, Shem was the first-born, and Japheth followed. When dealing with Noah's sons, the Table's order is Japheth first, Ham second, and Shem last. This kind of order-switching is characteristic of Genesis which reserves treating last the line through whom the Messiah was to come. Our primary concern in this study has to do with Ham and his descendants. It is Hamitic Black/African people who are our primary focus in our study of the Black presence in the Bible.

Following is a broad outline of each of the three main divisions of *Genesis 10*.

```
                    Table's Heading (1)


Japheth (2-5)         Ham (6-20)           Shem (21-31)


Heading (2)           Heading (6)            Pre-Heading (21)
Expansion (3-4)       Expansion (7)         Heading (22)
Colophon (5)          Colophon (20)         Expansion (23-29a)
                                             Colophon (Joktan,
                                                29b-30)
                                            Colophon (31)


                    Table's Colophon (32)
```

6. Its Composition, Sources, Date and Scope

We take the position that Moses composed the Table of Nations, *Genesis 10*. Moses was the author of the Pentateuch and he had been educated in all the wisdom of the Egyptians (Exodus 2:1-15; Acts 7:20, 29). As a prince of Egypt Moses would have had access to the vast amount of information reflected in the contents of the Table.

That Moses composed the Table does not necessitate that all the Table's contents originated with Moses. Apparently Moses sometimes compiled, sometimes wrote, sometimes edited information. As the Table has come down to us in its present written form, it probably underwent certain minor editorial work that was post-Moses.

The information in the Table is quite ancient. This is based both on its literary form and on its contents. The Table seems to reflect information much earlier than Moses which divided humanity into three grand divisions. In addition to Egyptian sources, Moses would have had information handed down to him through the Hebrew patriarchs. This information would have been written in Ur or its vicinity around 2000 B.C.

It was probably sometime within the second millennium B.C. that the Table was written (for the most part) into its present form. This dating is demonstrable by a number of ways,[77] not the least of which is the names which are mentioned in contrast to the names which are omitted. For example, the Hamitic "Sidon," is mentioned as the leading Phoenician city while "Tyre," nor "Phoenicia" is mentioned at all. This historical accuracy was true of the second millennium B.C., not of the first.

Within the Table's scope would be included peoples who were either 1) known to the ancient Egyptians (contemporarily or historically), and/or 2) known to the ancient Hebrews whose family histories, for the most part, provide the pattern for the Book of Genesis. It is probably the "known" world rather than the "entire" world indicated by "earth," when the Scripture reads, "These are the families of the sons of Noah, according to their genealogies, in their nations; and from these the nations spread abroad on the earth after the flood" (10:32). Thus, from the Table we can expect to see how the ancients viewed the presence of Hamitic Black/African peoples in their world, and perceive in some ways the spreading of these peoples throughout the known world.

C.

Understanding the Table's Structure

In what way is the Table of Nations put together? What characterizes its structure? The better one sees how this unique passage of Scripture has been fashioned, the better he/she can understand its names and the ancient historical relationships of the peoples they identify.

Following are several characteristics of the Table which have a bearing on any explanation of its names. This information is a digest and provided in concise form. We relate our findings primarily to Hamitic peoples.[78]

1. The Table is Genealogical

The Table of Nations, as mentioned above, is a genealogical table. The controlling genealogical term is the Hebrew word translated "generations" and "genealogies" (in verses 10:1 and 32, respectively). It means "history" and is used of "**genealogical history,**" of a family or the like.[79] Since the contents of the Table is couched between this genealogical term, the entire Table ought be understood in this context.

BIOLOGICAL

Genealogical primarily indicates **biological relationship;** blood-based kinship, ancestral heredity. Such relationships existed between peoples mentioned in the Table. Establishing the Black/African presence in the Scripture is in part founded upon showing actual physical/hereditary connections (the family tree) between ancient Black ancestors and their descendants. The Black presence in the Bible is more than cultural and conceptual. It is primarily ontological; it is Blackness in actual physical nature and being. It is the biological nature of Black peoples in *Genesis 10* which contributes toward substantiating this Biblical presence.

SEGMENTED

Two type of genealogies are found in ancient literature. The linear genealogy gives a single line of descent from an ancestor. The **segmented** genealogy, of which *Genesis 10* is one, describes more than one line of descent from an ancestor. It was used for different purposes including political, legal, domestic and religious purposes. It emphasized group interrelations over against individual relationships.

The segmentation of the Table is evident in the three branches of Noah's descendants (10:1, 2, 6, 21, 32). Perhaps the three branches at one time stood on their genealogical own prior to incorporation into the complete Table. It is evident that Ham's list (in contrast to the other two) reflects very ancient traditions.

Further segmentation of the Table is found within each branch. For instance, the genealogical line of three of Ham's descendants are given additional treatment (Cush, Egypt and Canaan, 10:8, 13, 15).

DESCENDING

Some genealogies look back, others forward. Some flow up, others down. Some emphasize ancestors, others descendants. Some ascend, others **descend**. *Genesis 10* is the descending type of genealogy. The original ancestor, that is Noah, is presented first. His most recent descendants (from the writer's perspective) are given last. (In contrast see Jesus' genealogy, Luke 3:23-38).

FORMULAIC

The Table is the genealogical type which uses technical **"formulas"** connecting its names. Following is a chart of the formulas used in *Genesis 10*.

"sons of"	"became the father of"	"children (sons) were born to"
Noah, 1		
Japheth (2)	Cush (8)	Noah's sons (1)
Gomer (3)	Egypt (13)	Shem (21)
Javan (4)	Canaan (15)	Eber (25)
Japheth (5)[80]	Arpachshad (24)	
Ham (6)	Shelah (24)	
Cush (7)	Joktan (26)	
Raamah (7)		
Ham (20)		
Shem (22)		
Aram (23)		
Joktan (29)		
Shem (31)		
Noah (32)		

The formulas "sons of" and "became the father of" are dominant in the Table, and each is used in reference to Hamitic peoples. "Sons of" is used of both the descendants of Ham (10:6), Cush (10:7a) and Raamah (10:7b). "Became the father of" is used of Nimrod (Cush's son, 10:8a), of Egypt, and of Canaan (Ham's sons, 10:13a, 15a).

Each formula is used to project is own area of concentration. "Sons of" points to the ancestor and stresses the beginning of the development. It gives the point of departure. It describes a situation, the state of being a nation. In contrast, "became the father of" points to the descendant and emphasizes the continuing results of the development. It describes how humankind spread over the earth and became the nations that they are. It shows the different ways in which different peoples developed.[81]

These genealogical formulas are relationship terms. Essentially they point to physical or kindred relationships, but do not stop there. They may also indicate social, cultural, and political relationships existing, not so much between individuals as between peoples and nations. Thus "son of" may be translated "descendant of," and may mean that the "son" has the **quality** of and is **dependent on** the ancestor. Likewise, "became the father of" may be translated "became the ancestor of," and may mean that "ancestor" is the **predecessor** or **founder** of the "son" and therefore is the **fountainhead** who **significantly impacts** the son.

Understood in this light, a "father" would be "a more powerful nation, a son was a dependent tribe, brothers were allies, daughters were suburbs."[82] For instance, when it is written that "Canaan became the father of Sidon" (Genesis 10:15), besides indicating ancestral relationship, it could also refer to a person (or land, or people) becoming the founder of a city. Or, take into consideration that "Egypt," a country, gives birth to "Ludim," a tribe (10:13).[83] Approaching the Table with this understanding frees the mind of the researcher to fully explore the nature of the relationships existing among the persons/peoples mentioned. There was definitely a hegemony—political, geographical, cultural, and social—existing between the peoples (and many Black peoples) mentioned in *Genesis 10*. The ties and dynamics existing between them were strong and multidimensional.

2. The Table's Names and Reports

Genesis 10, our "genealogical table," contains a variety of names. The style of names in the list is very creative. Yet, the Table contains more than names. It also has "notes." These notes serve as reports about several of the persons/people identified.

DIVERSE NAMES

The various names in the Table have been called "bewilderingly diverse." They include names of individuals, tribes, cities, inhabitants of those cities, and countries. Some of them are stylized and standardized. See for example the **"-im"** ending of names associated with Egypt (10:13), and the "-ite" ending of names associated with Canaan (10:16).

1) Four Categories of Names

The names listed in the Table of Nations were probably originally the names of 1) individuals which eventually came to be applied to 2) their descendants (these names are patronyms–names received from a paternal ancestor; that is, a clan/tribal name; for example, the descendants of "John" are called "Johnson."); and which in some cases came to be applied to 3) the territory which was inhabited by these people, and/or to 4) to the collective self-consciousness and governance of the people who considered themselves and were regarded by others as a nation.[84]

Thus, the names of *Genesis 10* include 1) **personal** names (including famous individuals); 2) **people** names (including clans and tribes); 3) **place** names (including well-known cities, regions, and lands); and 4) **political** names (those of great nations).

Below is a listing of several kinds of names found in the Table. They are all associated with the Hamitic genealogical line.

PERSONAL NAMES	PEOPLE NAMES
Ham (1)	Ludim (13)
Cush (8)	Caphtorim (13)
Nimrod (8)	Jebusites (16)
PLACE NAMES	**POLITICAL NAMES**
Babel (10, city)	Cush (6)
Shinar (10, region)	Egypt (6)[85]
Pathrusim (14, region)	Assyria (11)

2) An Ethnological Emphasis

In the midst of all its various names, the emphasis of the Table concerns ethnic entities, it is **ethnological.** Its primary concern is with "families," and "nations" (10:1, 5, 15, 20, 31, 32). Notice how the "Canaan" of verse 15a is extended to "the **families** of the Canaanites" in verse 15b. Also, some of the names regarded as individuals in *Genesis 10* are used as names of peoples in other historical settings and Biblical passages.

Many Biblical students explain the three major branches in the Table as comprehensive racial groupings of humanity; usually Negroid (Ham), Caucasoid (Japheth) and Mongoloid (Shem). However, despite these classifications, according to the actual terms employed, the two largest social divisions appearing in *Genesis 10* are "families," and "nations."[86] The term "race" does not appear within this passage of Scripture. Since this is the case, it would seem that the correct course of exposition would be to avoid the use of "race"/"racial" terminology, unless there are other reasons which warrant such a use.[87] The actual Biblical data must control our exegesis and exposition of the passage, not vice versa.[88]

An implication of viewing the Table's nature as ethnological rather than "racial" is that the presence of Black peoples is discoverable within the genealogical lines of other than descendants of Ham. For example, the Elamites, Shemitically listed (10:22), are a Black people according to anthropological studies of ancient peoples. Given an overall "racial" explanation of *Genesis 10*, this kind of identification would be impossible to make, or either the presence of the Elamites under Shem would be termed some kind of a misplacement.

In essence, *Genesis 10* is neither primarily individual nor racial, but ethnological. Expositions of the names in the Table must keep the ethnic context and dimension in mind.

3) Eponyms

Ofttimes a name appearing in the Table may be used in subsequent Biblical passages of a people. When this kind of usage occurs the named is called an "eponym," which the dictionary defines as "a person, real or imaginary, from whom something, as a tribe, nation or place, takes or is said to take its name." For example, "Israel" is the name of a person (formerly known as "Jacob") and the name of a nation ("the children of Israel"). This use indicates an eponym who is "real." This is how we use the term "eponymous" in this treatment. It refers to an actual person, not to a mythical, mystical or imaginary person.[89]

REPORTS

There are "reports" attached to at least seven names in the Table. These "notes" provide information about the persons/people named and their descendants. The information provided is of an historical nature. Four of the seven notes relate to Hamitic peoples: **Nimrod** (10:8b-12), **Philistines** (10:14), **Sidon** (10:15), and the **Canaanites** (10:18b-19). It is worth noting that the Cushite Nimrod report is the longest and most complex in the Table. Nimrod was an exceptional Black person of antiquity.

3. The Table's Multidimensional Nature

THE COLOPHONS

Several "**colophons**" appear throughout the Table. These colophons serve as summaries or conclusions to the Table as a whole, and to each individual branch (10:5, 20, 31, 32). From the colophons the reader understands the multidimensional nature of the Table. It is reflected in the "families" of the "descendants" (or "sons") of Noah according to their "genealogies" in their "nations," and from these (from either the "families" or from the "nations" composing the families) the "nations" spread abroad on the "earth" following the Flood. This is the summary of the Table in verse 32. From the sub-sections we also learn that the Table's names are criteriarized "with reference to" their "families" and their "languages" (or "tongues"), even "each with his own language" (in Japheth's case), and in their "lands" and their "nations." Further, of Japheth it is said that "from these the coastland peoples spread." This information is received from Genesis 10:1, 5, 20, 31, and 32.[90]

Thus, in the Table of Nations, we learn of:

The **genealogies** (lines of descent) within the **nations** of Noah's
  son's (or descendant's)
  families (clans).

This information is presented according to
  1) their **families** (clans);
  2) the **languages** they spoke;
  3) the **lands** in which they lived; and
  4) the **nations** to which they belonged.

These **families** (clans) and/or **nations** spread abroad
  1) on the **earth**
  2) on the **coastlands**

  following the Flood.

FOUR-FOLD DIVISION

The multidimensional nature of the Table is four-fold. *Genesis 10* has to do with "families," "languages," "lands," and "nations." Therefore, the divisions reflected in the Table are **ethnological**, **linguistic**, **geographical**, and **political**. It was according to this criteria that names were selected and/or organized into the Table.

MOVEMENT AND INTERMIXTURE OF PEOPLES

Intermixture among peoples is indicated in the Table through the same name which appears under two different branches. The reader will discover that among both Ham's and Shem's descendants we find the names "Havilah," "Sheba," "Assyria" ("Asshur"), and "Ludim" ("Lud") (see 10:7, 11, 13, 22, 28, 29).

Ancient peoples moved and were moved upon. They drifted, migrated, infiltrated, or conquered.[91] Their names could have different meanings under different circumstances. These peoples mixed and co-mingled. They intermarried. Matching names between the Table and peoples identified in extra-Biblical sources hinges in part upon the correlation of historical situations reported in the Bible with historical events in the world of the Bible.[92]

What the reader shall discover is that Hamitic people were foundational, and their presence in the ancient world impacted people all over. The movements of peoples would also account for African people spreading throughout the continent of Africa, and even spreading throughout the world! Black American people, stolen by Europeans from the African continent, are one of the Black groups descended from the people of Cush.

SECTION V

Ham and Hamitic Descendants

A.   Ham: The Father of Black/African Peoples

B.   Understanding "Hamitic"

C.   The Sons/Descendants of Ham

D.   The Cushites

E.   Mizraim (Egypt)

F.   The Putites

G.   The Canaanites

H.   How Can Ham be "Black" and

His Brothers not?

I.   The Blackness of Original Humanity

and Prototypical Civilizations

A.

Ham: The Father of Black/African Peoples

Ham was the middle child of Noah's three sons, "Shem, Ham, and Japheth" (Genesis 5:32; 6:10; 7:13; 9:18, 22; 10:1, 6, 20; 1 Chronicles 1:4, 8). The name "Ham" means "hot," "heat," and by application, "black."[93]

Ham was the only son of Noah after whom a country/nation was named. Concerning neither Shem nor Japheth was there a Biblical people who could claim either as their namesake. The name "Ham" is patronymic of his descendants. That is, it is a name received from a paternal ancestor. With reference to the people of Ham the son of Noah, "Ham" is found several other times in the Scripture (1 Chronicles 4:40; Psalm 78:51; 105:23; 105:27; 106:22).

1. Ham is Mizraim (Egypt)

According to the references in the Psalms, Ham is synonymous with Egypt. Psalm 78:51 speaks of God smiting the first-born in Egypt which it parallels with the "tents of Ham." Psalm 105:23 and 27 speak again of Egypt being the "land of Ham," which served as the place of Joseph's sojourn and Moses' miracles. Psalm 106:22 speaks also of the "land of Ham," where the reference is to the Israelites who forgot the wondrous works which God their Savior had done for them in Egypt (v. 21).

It is clear from the parallel Hebrew poetry of the Psalms that Ham is Egypt in Africa. It is at this point that the Bible stands in stark contrast to those scholars who do not want to associate Egypt, Africa with Black peoples. The Biblical writers had no problem with such an association, for they knew the ancient records.

2. Ham is a Place in Canaan

Yet, "Ham," has also another Biblical meaning. Besides Egypt, "Ham" is also a place located in the land of Canaan. This usage is found in Genesis 14:5 and also 1 Chronicles 4:40. According to the former reference, Ham in Canaan was located in Transjordan (east of the Jordan) and served as the home of a people called the Zuzim.[94] It was in this territory that the Elamite king Chedorlaomer, and the kings with him, defeated the people of Zuzim.

First Chronicles 4:40 is most enlightening. This verse indicates that the people of Ham positively affected their environment to the extent that their land was rich, good pastureland; it was very broad, quiet and peaceful "...for the former inhabitants there belonged to Ham." The descendants of Simeon came to live in this Hamitic territory when the Israelite nation came to conquer and settle Canaan land (cf. 1 Chronicles 4:24-43). Ancient Black people took care of their community, such is the witness of Scripture.

3. Ham is the Aboriginal heart of Mizraim (Egypt)

In addition to "Ham" being both a patronymic designation for Egypt, Africa, and for a place in Canaan's Transjordan, it may also be the designation of a people who were the most ancient core group of the people of Egypt. This designation would be arrived at by an exposition of Genesis 10:6: "The sons of Ham:...Mizraim" (*NIV*).

"Ham" is apparently not used as a strict designation for Mizraim in Genesis 10:6. It would not make much sense to say that the son/descendant of "Mizraim" was "Mizraim." It would however be appropriate to say that the son/descendant of Ham (a person) was "Mizraim." However, the Scripture seems to become most clear when we understand it to say that the the son/descendant of "Ham" (the aboriginal people and heart of Egypt) was "Mizraim" ("the two red mud lands"; a reference to Upper and Lower Egypt).[95]

In summary, "Ham," the person, is the ancestor of "Ham," his people (both in Canaan and in the aboriginal heart of Egypt), who are the ancestors of "Mizraim" (Lower and Upper Egypt). Such an understanding of these verses concurs with the historical and other studies pointing to Egypt's Nile Valley as the birthplace of humanity and civilization.[96]

B.

Understanding "Hamitic"

The term "Hamitic" refers to the descendants of Ham. In the past many scholars began to apply the term Hamitic to language, particularly in reference to non-Semitic branches of the Afroasiatic language family. Then a subtle switch occurred. Some scholars began to apply the term Hamitic, not only to language, but also to race or ethnic group. This same procedure also took place in reference to the descendants of Shem, known as "Semitic" people.[97]

The application of the terms "Hamitic" or "Semitic" to language as well as to ancestry left many people confused about Black peoples. Why? Because not all "Semitic speaking" people are non-Hamitic people. For instance, the Phoenicians, who spoke Semitically, are descendants of Ham.[98] Moreover, Canaanite people are genealogically related to Ham, not Shem. The Bible classifies the Canaanites as a Hamitic people, an explicitly Black people, despite the fact that according to language studies "Canaanite" describes "the non-Aramaic group of first-millennium languages that are part of the Northwest Semitic family, principally Phoenician and Hebrew (cf. Isaiah 18:19)."[99] Many sources give the Canaanite people a primary "Semitic" identification. In such a case, one must choose to go by what the Bible teaches when demonstrating ancestral connections between ancient Black peoples; not by "Webster's Dictionary," modern language studies, or any other source pursuing a similar line of thought.[100]

In this regard we read in reference to "Hamitic": "In the biblical sense, however, genetic descent is all that is implied, and with the movement and intermarriage of peoples and the changes of language which took place in ancient times common descent from Ham would not necessarily imply common habitat, language, or even race in a recognizable form."[101]

The Text of Genesis 10:1, 6-20

Following is a listing of the portion of Scripture from *Genesis 10* related to the Hamitic genealogical line. It is from the *RSV* and has been stylized in such a way as to promote its study.

Genesis 10:1

These are the generations of the sons of Noah, Shem, **Ham,** and Japheth; sons were born to them after the flood.

Genesis 10:6-20

{6} The sons of **Ham:**
   Cush, Egypt, Put, and Canaan.

   {7} The sons of **Cush:**
      Seba, Havilah, Sabtah, Raamah, and Sabteca.
         The sons of Raamah: Sheba and Dedan.

   {8} **Cush** became the father of
      Nimrod;
      he was the first on earth to be a mighty man. {9} He was a mighty hunter before the LORD; therefore it is said, "Like Nimrod a mighty hunter before the LORD."

      {10} The beginning of his kingdom was Babel, Erech, and Accad, all of them in the land of Shinar.

      {11} From that land he went into Assyria, and built Nineveh, Rehoboth-Ir, Calah, and {12} Resen
         between Nineveh and Calah;
      that is the great city.

{13} **Egypt** became the father of
Ludim, Anamim, Lehabim, Naphtuhim, {14} Pathrusim, Casluhim
(whence came the Philistines),
and Caphtorim.

{15} **Canaan** became the father of
Sidon
his first-born, and
Heth, {16} and

the Jebusites, the Amorites, the Girgashites, {17} the Hivites, the Arkites, the Sinites, {18} the Arvadites, the Zemarites, and the Hamathites.

Afterward the **families of the Canaanites**
spread abroad.

{19} And the **territory of the Canaanites**
extended from Sidon, in the direction of Gerar, as far as Gaza, and in the direction of Sodom, Gomorrah, Admah, and Zeboiim, as far as Lasha.

{20} These are the sons of Ham,
by their families,
their languages,
their lands, and
their nations.

The Hamitic Black/African Genealogical Line

Following is a chart of the Hamitic Black/African genealogical line based on Genesis 10. It is traced through the names presented in the passage, all which indicate males.

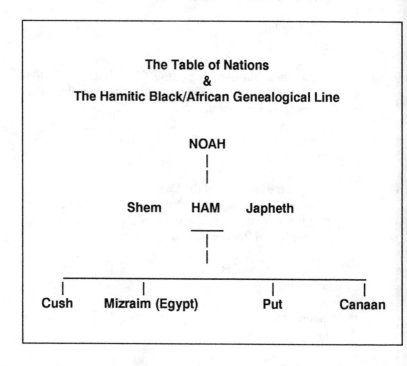

The Table of Nations
&
The Hamitic Black/African Genealogical Line

NOAH

Shem   HAM   Japheth

Cush   Mizraim (Egypt)   Put   Canaan

The Hamites had more contact with the Israelites than did the Japhethites (from whom white people are descended). Ham and his descendants settled (for the most part) in northern Africa and western Asia.[102]

C.

The Sons/Descendants of Ham

An Overview

There is common agreement among most scholars that Ham, Noah's second born according to Genesis 5:32 and 1 Chronicles 1:4, was the father of indigenous African peoples. This identification is popularly held by scholars of ancient history who have an interest in Biblical studies, as well as by those scholars who profess little interest in the Biblical message. When we take an historical, cultural and anthropological look at the descendants which sprang from Ham, we cannot help but discover that they possess the kind of evident degree of Blackness which overshadows any evident Black ethnicity of Noah's other son's descendants, the Semites and Japhethites.

There are ample Biblical references to the Cushites, Egyptians, and the Canaanites. Each of these Hamitic descendants is clearly historically and geographically identifiable as a specific people. There is less Biblical information about Put, and the researchers identify his descendants as either of two peoples: the people of Libya or Somaliland.[103] Nevertheless, this son/descendant of Ham is clearly identified in the Scripture with other African countries and so situated in the same geographical area on the continent of Africa.

It is interesting to note that Ham's descendants affected and influenced the Hebrew-Israelite-Judahite people more than any other nation in the Old Testament. These descendants would include the Egyptians, Canaanites, Babylonians and others. Their impact on the Covenant people of God was tremendous.

The Evident Degree of Blackness of Ham's Sons

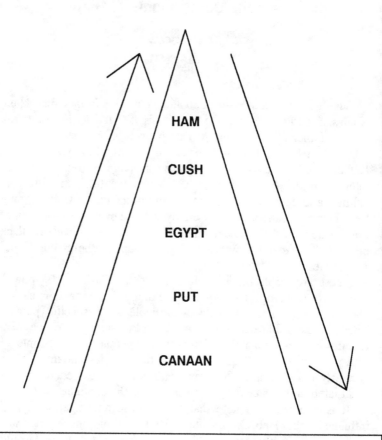

Up the pyramid the descendants of Ham become more obviously Black. Geographically, Canaan is furthest north, while Cush is furthest south into Africa. Down the pyramid the descendants of Ham are less obviously Black. Here we speak only of what is "obvious," of what is perceptible. "Blackness" constitutes more than perception. Blackness is also that which is ancestrally inherited, regardless of the degree of skin pigmentation. Witness the many fair shades of Black Americans.

Identifying Ham's Sons

Biblically, Historically, and Geographically

HAM

CUSH	EGYPT	PUT	CANAAN
Biblical Info.	Biblical Info.	Biblical Info.	Biblical Info.
Historically And Geographically Identifiable	Historically And Geographically Identifiable	Either of two Specific Nations.	Historically And Geographically Identifiable

**But Always
Clearly Identified
With African Countries and so
Situated in the Same Area.**

D.

The Cushites

Genesis 10:7

The sons of Cush: Seba, Havilah, Sabtah, Raamah, and Sabteca. The sons of Raamah: Sheba and Dedan.

Genesis 10:8-12

{8} Cush became the father of Nimrod; he was the first on earth to be a mighty man. {9} He was a mighty hunter before the LORD; therefore it is said, "Like Nimrod a mighty hunter before the LORD." {10} The beginning of his kingdom was Babel, Erech, and Accad, all of them in the land of Shinar. {11} From that land he went into Assyria, and built Nineveh, Rehoboth-Ir, Calah, and {12} Resen between Nineveh and Calah; that is the great city.

1. Overview

As we look at the Biblical data we discover that Cush is the first-mentioned descendant of Ham (Genesis 10:6). Furthermore, as we look at the entire Table of Nations we notice that Cush and his descendants stand out among the other descendants of Ham as well as among the other descendants of Noah mentioned in the branches of Shem and Japheth.

For instance, as we examine the information about Japheth we discover that four verses concern him and his descendants (Genesis 10:2-5). The information about Shem and his descendants is contained in 11 verses (Genesis 10:21-31). In contrast, the information about Ham and his descendants is contained in 15 verses (Genesis 10:6-20).

Then, if we compare the information about Cush to the other descendants of Ham we find the following. Cush's descendants are spoken of in six verses (Genesis 10:7-12). Mizraim's (Egypt's) descendants are spoken of in two verses (Genesis 10:13-14). There is no mention of any descendants of Put. Canaan's descendants are dealt with in five verses (Genesis 10:15-19).

Finally if we take a look at Nimrod, the sixth son of Cush, we discover that he alone is spoken about in 5 verses (Genesis 10:15-19).

This allocation of space to Ham's descendants, especially to Cush, suggests a position of power and importance, prosperity and dominance.[104] Inasmuch as the Bible does not deal with history and genealogy for their own importance, it can be safely concluded that extensive treatment of Ham's and Cush's descendants represents some weighty significance for the Scripture and its purpose as a whole.[105]

2. Cushite Descendants

In addition to the descendants of Cush, which nation continued to bear the name of their paternal ancestor and developed into a great civilization south of Egypt, Cush is identified with other descendants who did not bear his name. Notice that Genesis 10:6-7 provides the names of Cush's descendants. They are called, "Seba," "Havilah," "Sabtah," "Raamah," "Sabteca," and "Nimrod." Cush's descendants through Raamah were "Sheba" and "Dedan." Excluding Nimrod, the seven descendants (five sons and two grandsons) of Cush are mostly located in Arabia or in Africa close to Arabia.

SEBA

It is possible that the people of Seba, the Sabeans, are to be identified with more than one place in the ancient world. It has been identified both with Meroe in Upper Egypt and Sheba in South

Arabia. Seba was an important trading center. In the following verses it is linked with Cush and Egypt:

Isaiah 43:3   For I am the LORD your God, the Holy One of Israel, your Savior. I give Egypt as your ransom, Ethiopia and Seba in exchange for you.

Isaiah 45:14   Thus says the LORD: "The wealth of Egypt and the merchandise of Ethiopia, and the Sabeans, men of stature, shall come over to you and be yours, they shall follow you; they shall come over in chains and bow down to you. They will make supplication to you, saying: 'God is with you only, and there is no other, no god besides him.'"

Seba is linked with Sheba in the following verse:

Psalm 72:10   May the kings of Tarshish and of the isles render him tribute, may the kings of Sheba and Seba bring gifts!

According to Job 1:14, 15 it was the Sabeans who raided Job's oxen and killed his servants.

HAVILAH

Havilah, whose name is rooted in "sandy," cannot be identified with precision. There were a number of sandy places in Arabia. In the Scripture Havilah may be used in regard to the entire land of Arabia. According to the following verses Havilah is associated with one of the rivers associated with the Garden in Eden:

Genesis 2:11, 12   The name of the first is Pishon; it is the one which flows around the whole land of Havilah, where there is gold; and the gold of that land is good; bdellium and onyx stone are there.

SABTAH

Sabtah has been identified with Sabota in Arabia, the chief city of the land of Hadramaut (the Hazarmaveth of Genesis 10:26). Sabtah was an old commercial city whose people were famed for trading in incense. Sabtah is mentioned one other time in the Scripture: 1 Chronicles 1:9, the other genealogical passage parallel to the Table.

RAAMAH

Several suggestions have been put forth for locating Raamah. A strong possibility is that this tribe was located in southwestern Arabia near Ma'an. According to the following verse (and its context) the merchants of Raamah and Sheba traded with Tyre their spices, precious stones, and gold:

Ezekiel 27:22 The traders of Sheba and Raamah traded with you; they exchanged for your wares the best of all kinds of spices, and all precious stones, and gold.

Raamah's descendants were Sheba and Dedan. Each of these sons have multiple and diverse listings in the Scripture.

SHEBA, son of Raamah

As used in Scripture, the name Sheba apparently refers to two or three different progenitors of one or more Arabian tribes and/or places. As a Hamitic descendant, Sheba is a reference to Saba and are the Sabaeans in Yemen, southwest Arabia. They were a rich people and their home a land of extensive commerce. They exported gold, frankincense, and other valuables.

Isaiah 60:6 A multitude of camels shall cover you, the young camels of Midian and Ephah; all those from Sheba shall come. They shall bring gold and frankincense, and shall proclaim the praise of the LORD.

Jeremiah 6:20 To what purpose does frankincense come to me from Sheba, or sweet cane from a distant land? Your burnt offerings are not acceptable, nor your sacrifices pleasing to me.

The **Queen of Sheba** has been a most notable figure within and outside Biblical history. The visit of this powerful and beautiful Black woman to king Solomon is recorded in 1 Kings 10:1-13. Josephus says that she was the Queen of Egypt and Ethiopia.[106]

DEDAN, son of Raamah

Dedan was located in northwestern Arabia along the Red Sea. It was an important tribe controlling caravan routes between South and North Arabia.

Ezekiel 38:13 Sheba and Dedan and the merchants of Tarshish and all its villages will say to you, 'Have you come to seize spoil? Have you assembled your hosts to carry off plunder, to carry away silver and gold, to take away cattle and goods, to seize great spoil?'

Isaiah 21:13 The oracle concerning Arabia. In the thickets in Arabia you will lodge, O caravans of Dedanites.

SABTECA

This fifth son/descendant of Cush is mentioned only here and in 1 Chronicles 1:9. "Sabteca" is thought to have passed on to a southeastern Arabian locality. Interesting is the assertion that

Sabteca is considered etymologically by some in relation to the Nubian Pharaoh Hebiktu (Shabataka).[107]

NIMROD

Nimrod is the sixth and most notable son of Cush. The first report of the Table is attached to his name (10:8b-11). Through this narrative we learn about Nimrod's personal achievements, his proverbial legendary status, his kingdom's foundation and its expansion.[108]

Many noble suggestions have been given trying to establish the identity of Nimrod outside the Scripture. These attempts have been elusive. Accepting Nimrod as an individual descendant of Cush is Biblically sufficient. Nimrod was one of our great Black ancestors. Following is a listing which may assist us in capturing the character and work of Nimrod based on Genesis 10:8-11.

1) Nimrod was a Creative Pioneer
He is viewed as the "first" on earth to be a mighty man (compare other "firsts" in Genesis 4:26; 6:1; 9:20).

2) Nimrod was a Liberator
He was a "mighty man," a "champion;" he was a "champion hunter," "a champion of game." Nimrod delivered the community from man-slaying beasts. He was a social activist.

3) Nimrod was Spiritual
His actions and activities were done "before the Lord." He maintained a sense of the presence of God, to whom he was accountable.

4) Nimrod was Legendary
People would proclaim to their children, young people, adults – to anyone who would excel – "(May you be) like Nimrod a mighty hunter before the Lord." Through his acts of deliverance,

Nimrod earned a great reputation. His life was worthy of emulation.

5) Nimrod was a King

Through his acts of deliverance, Nimrod ascended into the kingship. His kingdom was the offspring of his acts of deliverance and spiritual character. He was a servant-leader.

6) Nimrod was a Kingdom Builder

His kingdom was anchored by building, not conquering, great cities such as Babel, Erech, Accad, and Calneh[109] in Babylonia, "the land of Shinar." His building was an achievement in excellence. "The beginning" has both chronological and qualitative significance.[110] He built "great" cities.

7) Nimrod was Progressive

The righteous self-determination of Nimrod led him to bring the benefits of his kingdom into the land of Assyria. He made progress, and others benefited by his progress. There is not one hint that Nimrod was violent or oppressed other peoples. Instead he "built" Nineveh, Rehoboth-Ir, Calah and Resen – all Assyrian cities.

3. Summary

The first seven descendants of Cush are situated in Arabia or Africa close to Arabia. The sixth Cushite descendant, Nimrod, establishes the Cushite presence in southwestern Asia, both in Babylonia ("the land of Shinar") in southern Mesopotamia, and then up the Tigris-Euphrates rivers into Assyria, northern Mesopotamia.

Of special interest in this treatment of Cushite descendants whose ancient presence in the Biblical world was extensive would be "the land of Shinar." This phrase is a definite reference to the ancient people known as the Sumerians. The Sumerians were composed of people who were the indigenous population of Mesopotamia and called themselves "the blackheads." Their origin was Cushite.   "Shinar" is mentioned several times in the Old Testament (Genesis 11:2; 14:1, 9; Joshua 7:21; Isaiah 11:1; Zechariah 5:11; Daniel 1:2).

Daniel 1:1-4 shows the relationship between "Babylon," the "land of Shinar," and the "Chaldeans."

{1} In the third year of the reign of Jehoiakim king of Judah, Nebuchadnezzar king of **Babylon** came to Jerusalem and besieged it. {2} And the Lord gave Jehoiakim king of Judah into his hand, with some of the vessels of the house of God; and he brought them to the **land of Shinar,** to the house of his god, and placed the vessels in the treasury of his god. {3} Then the king commanded Ashpenaz, his chief eunuch, to bring some of the people of Israel, both of the royal family and of the nobility, {4} youths without blemish, handsome and skilful in all wisdom, endowed with knowledge, understanding learning, and competent to serve in the king's palace, and to teach them the letters and language of the **Chaldeans.**

The "Chaldeans" should be classified as Biblical Blacks.   King Nebuchadnezzar would qualify,   so would Merodoch-baladan (2 Kings 20:12; Isaiah 39:1), Evil-merodach (2 Kings 25:27; Jeremiah 52:31), and Belshazzar (Daniel 5:1, 30).

E.

Mizraim (Egypt)

Genesis 10:13-14

Egypt became the father of Ludim, Anamim, Lehabim, Naphtuhim, {14} Pathrusim, Casluhim (whence came the Philistines), and Caphtorim.

1. Overview

The student of the Scripture well understands that Egypt, Africa, as a great Black nation, played a most important role in connection with the Israelite people. Matter of fact, Egypt, Africa formed the contextual civilization which for hundreds of years affected the development of the Israelite cultural experience. Perhaps no other people save the Canaanites affected the Israelite nation like their southern neighbor, Egypt, Africa. A numerical picture may be helpful. Throughout the *Revised Standard Version* "Egypt" appears 617 times, "Egypt's" 3 times, "Egyptian" 24 times, "Egyptian's" 3 times, and "Egyptians" 103 times.

Egypt, Africa is intertwined in this subject of the Black presence in the Scripture. Its significance will be highlighted as our discussion develops.

2. Mizraim's (Egypt's) Descendants

For now, we will briefly consider the descendants of Egypt, as described in *Genesis 10*. The listing provides information about Egypt herself as well as about peoples having connections with Egypt. Egypt's descendants are the "Ludim," "Anamim," "Lehabim,"

"Naphtuhim," "Pathrusim," "Casluhim," "the Philistines" (an offshoot), and "Caphtorim." Geographically, the identifiable names range from northern Africa to the eastern Mediterranean.

LUDIM

The Ludim cannot be identified with certainty. They may be related to Lud in Shem's line (Genesis 10:22). It would appear they lived in north Africa, in or near Egypt. If Ludim = Lud, then the verses below associate them with Ethiopia, Put, Arabia, and all Libya; but also with Persia, located in a different geographical locale. We also learn that they served as mercenaries in the Egyptian army (Jeremiah 46:9; Ezekiel 30:5).

Jeremiah 46:9 Advance, O horses, and rage, O chariots! Let the warriors go forth: men of Ethiopia and Put who handle the shield, men of Lud, skilled in handling the bow.

Ezekiel 27:10 "Persia and Lud and Put were in your army as your men of war; they hung the shield and helmet in you; they gave you splendor.

Ezekiel 30:5 Ethiopia, and Put, and Lud, and all Arabia, and Libya, and the people of the land that is in league, shall fall with them by the sword.

Isaiah 66:19 associates Lud with Asia Minor. To Josephus, Lud is the Lydians of Asia Minor, who were called *Luddu* by the Assyrians. They were Hamitic.[111]

ANAMIM

The Anamim are not specifically identifiable. Suggestions have been put forth for a location in Cyrene, in Egypt west of Alexandria, and in the Nile Delta.

LEHABIM

The Lehabim may be related to the "Lubim," the Libyans. They lived in the desert region of northern Africa west of the Nile valley. According to Nahum 3:9; and Jeremiah 46:7-9, the Libyans are associated with Ethiopia and Egypt.

Nahum 3:9 Ethiopia was her strength, Egypt too, and that without limit; Put and the Libyans were her helpers.

Jeremiah 46:7-9 {7} "Who is this, rising like the Nile, like rivers whose waters surge? {8} Egypt rises like the Nile, like rivers whose waters surge. He said, I will rise, I will cover the earth, I will destroy cities and their inhabitants. {9} Advance, O horses, and rage, O chariots! Let the warriors go forth: men of Ethiopia and Put who handle the shield, men of Lud, skilled in handling the bow.

Libyans were among the forces of Shishak (2 Chronicles 12:3) and Zerah the Ethiopian (2 Chronicles 16:8; 14:9).

NAPHTUHIM

Amidst several suggestions, the Naphtuhim is probably a reference to the people of Lower Egypt, in the north. Thus it would balance the people mentioned next.

PATHRUSIM

Pathrusim means "an inhabitant of Pathros." This is a reference to Upper Egypt, and means "the Southland." In the following verses Pathros is associated with Memphis, and Zoan (Tanis), both cities in southern Egypt.

Jeremiah 44:1 The word that came to Jeremiah concerning all the Jews that dwelt in the land of Egypt, at Migdol, at Tahpanhes, at Memphis, and in the land of Pathros,

Ezekiel 30:14 I will make Pathros a desolation, and will set fire to Zoan, and will execute acts of judgment upon Thebes.

Note the sequence of north to south African geographical locations in the following verse.

Isaiah 11:11 In that day the Lord will extend his hand yet a second time to recover the remnant which is left of his people, from Assyria, from **Egypt, from Pathros, from Ethiopia,** from Elam, from Shinar, from Hamath, and from the coastlands of the sea.

Pathros was the native home of the Egyptians according to Ezekiel 29:13-16, a prophecy indicating that God would restore the fortunes of Egypt while restoring them from being scattered to their homeland where they would eventually come to know that, says God, "I am the Lord God."

CASLUHIM

The Casluhim have yet to be identified with certainty. Several suggestions have been made for their geographical identity inside as well as outside Egypt.

The PHILISTINES, Casluhim offshoot

At this point the second Hamitic "report" is attached to the Casluhim. They are the people "whence came the Philistines" (Genesis 10:14b). Apparently the Philistines were one of the Sea Peoples who came from the islands of the Aegean Sea regions and invaded and/or migrated into Palestine in the 13th century B.C. They came from Crete or by way of Crete into Canaan. Yet, much earlier the Philistines were living in Canaan. Both Abraham and Isaac sojourned among the Philistines of Canaan (Genesis 20-21; 26). According to the following passage the Philistines are associated with several of their familiar city-states, the Mediterranean, the Cherethites, and the land of Canaan.

> **Zephaniah 2:4-7** {4} For Gaza shall be deserted, and Ashkelon shall become a desolation; Ashdod's people shall be driven out at noon, and Ekron shall be uprooted. {5} Woe to you **inhabitants of the seacoast,** you nation of the **Cherethites!** The word of the LORD is against you, **O Canaan, land of the Philistines;** and I will destroy you till no inhabitant is left. {6} And you, **O seacoast,** shall be pastures, meadows for shepherds and folds for flocks. {7} The **seacoast** shall become the possession of the remnant of the house of Judah, on which they shall pasture, and in the houses of Ashkelon they shall lie down at evening. For the LORD their God will be mindful of them and restore their fortunes.

Among David's fighting forces were to be found Philistines, known as the Cherethites, the Pelethites, and the Gittites.

> **2 Samuel 15:18** And all his servants passed by him; and all the Cherethites, and all the Pelethites, and all the six hundred Gittites who had followed him from Gath, passed on before the king.

Besides the fact that Egypt had very early contact with the "Sea People," "Crete," and the "Philistines,"[112] another reason the Philistines are associated with Egypt is because the Philistines had been settling along the coastal highway to Egypt.

CAPHTORIM

The Caphtorim lived outside Egypt. Caphtor is a definite reference to the Island of Crete. The Aegean area including Crete had definite and early contact with Libya and Egypt. Crete, though not all Black, had explicit Black people in its population, and its roots were Black.[113] Blacks from Egypt came to Crete to serve as auxiliaries.[114] According to Acts 2:11 Cretans were present at Pentecost, and the book of Titus is addressed to those living on this island.

Acts 2:11 Cretans and Arabians, we hear them telling in our own tongues the mighty works of God."

Titus 1:4-5 {4} To Titus, my true child in a common faith: Grace and peace from God the Father and Christ Jesus our Savior. {5} This is why I left you in Crete, that you might amend what was defective, and appoint elders in every town as I directed you,

3. Summary

The seven tribes and one offshoot of Egypt show the extended relationship of their "father" to these descendants. Mizraim became the ancestor of these peoples, whether located inside or outside Egypt. They were derived from and dependent on Mizraim.

F.

The Putites

Genesis 10:6

The sons of Ham: Cush, Egypt, Put, and Canaan.

Put is the third son/descendant of Ham, the only one with no descendants named in the Table. Such omission is an indication of the "telescoping" nature of the Table. By name Put is mentioned eight times in the Bible (Genesis 10:6; 1 Chronicles 1:8; Isaiah 66:19; Jeremiah 46:9; Ezekiel 27:10; 30:5; 38:5; Nahum 3:9). According to Josephus, Put was the founder of Libya, whose inhabitants were called the Putites.[115] The Septuagint translates Put into "Libya." Libya is located in northern Africa west of Egypt. Other scholars identify Put with the *Punt* of an Egyptian inscription in East African Somaliland.[116]

Shishak (Sheshonq I, ca. 945-915 B.C.) was an Egyptian pharaoh of Libyan origin, and founder of the Twenty-second Dynasty (ca. 945-7:30). He is mentioned in 1 Kings 11:40; 14:25; 2 Chronicles 12:2ff. in relations with Jeroboam I (providing him refuge), and with Rehoboam (invading Palestine).

G.

The Canaanites

Genesis 10:15-19

{15} Canaan became the father of Sidon his first-born, and Heth, {16} and the Jebusites, the Amorites, the Girgashites, {17} the Hivites, the Arkites, the Sinites, {18} the Arvadites, the Zemarites, and the Hamathites. Afterward the families of the Canaanites spread abroad. {19} And the territory of the Canaanites extended from Sidon, in the direction of Gerar, as far as Gaza, and in the direction of Sodom, Gomorrah, Admah, and Zeboiim, as far as Lasha.

1. Overview

Canaan was the fourth son/descendant of Ham. His people were generally known as the Canaanites. Their land was known as Canaan.

The name Canaan has been understood by some to mean "belonging to (the land of) Purple."[117] However, the name "Canaanite," as used in several Bible passages, denotes a "trader," "merchant."[118] This could be expected because their most characteristic occupation was trading, and in particular, trading in purple dye. "...it may not be far from the truth that the use of the word 'Canaanite' for a merchant class is older than its use for the land and its population...In any case, the name became identified with the people who were the merchants par excellence of the ancient world."[119]

"Canaanites" are the persons who inhabited the land preceding the Israelite occupation, and their cultural inheritors. In its wider sense, "Canaanites" refers to different ethnic entities coming under its umbrella. In a narrower sense, "Canaanites" refers to one specific ethnic entity who lived in Canaan (see Genesis 34:30; Numbers 13:29; Deuteronomy 7:1; Joshua 5:1; 11:3). They lived in the area that was "always the heartland of the culture, the coastal region including its natural extension into the Jezreel Valley and the Jordan area."[120] In the days of the Judges, Jabin was "king of Canaan" (Judges 4:2, 23, 24.)

2. Canaanite Descendants

Two First-Fruit Canaanites

SIDON

Sidon is a reference to the Phoenicians who inhabited the narrow region along the northeastern Mediterranean coast. It was one of the familiar Phoenician city-states. The "report" attached to Sidon says that he was the "first-born" of Canaan. In the second millennium B.C. Sidon held the prominent position among Phoenician city-states. Tyre, "the daughter of Sidon" (Isaiah 23:12), the other familiar Phoenician city-state, gained prominence only in the time of David and Solomon. Ethbaal, the father of Jezebel, was king of the Sidonians according to 1 Kings 16:31. The Syro-Phoenician woman whose daughter was healed by Jesus was from the region of Tyre and Sidon (Mark 7:24-31). According to the following passage many Sidonians were receptive to the teaching and healing ministry of Jesus.

Luke 6:17-19 {17} And he came down with them and stood on a level place, with a great crowd of his disciples and a great multitude of people from all Judea and Jerusalem and the seacoast of Tyre and Sidon, who came to hear him and to be healed of their diseases; {18} and those who were troubled with unclean spirits were cured. {19} And all the crowd sought to touch him, for power came forth from him and healed them all.

HETH

Heth, the second first-fruit Canaanite, is a reference to the Hittites of Canaan. They should be distinguished from the Indo-European Hittites of Asia Minor who bore the same name. The Hittites were the indigenous "people of the land" of Canaan (Genesis 23:12, 13) in which Abraham and Isaac sojourned. They lived in the central ridge of Judah, especially the Hebron district. Uriah, the husband of Bathsheba, was a Hittite (2 Samuel 11:3); so was Tidal king of Goiim (Genesis 14:1) whose name is Hittite. Esau's wives Judith and Basemath were also Hittite women (Genesis 27:46; 26:34f.).

Four Familiar Canaanites

We call four of the Canaanites "familiar" because their names appear regularly in the lists of seven nations whom Israel was to dispossess from Canaan. See Deuteronomy 7:1; Joshua 3:10; 24:11; 1 Chronicles 1:14.

THE JEBUSITES

The Jebusites were the inhabitants who lived in and around Jebus, Jerusalem. They lived in the hill country of Canaan in the vicinity of Jerusalem at the time of the conquest (Numbers 13:29; Joshua 3:10; 11:3). Melchizedek, king of Salem (which later became Jerusalem), would have been the earliest ruler of Jebusite territory (Genesis 14:18ff.). Adonizedek is the second king of Jebus mentioned in the Old Testament (Joshua 10:1ff.). According to the following verses from Ezekiel, the indigenous population of Jerusalem was Hittite and Amorite.

Ezekiel 16:3 and say, Thus says the Lord GOD to Jerusalem: Your origin and your birth are of the land of the Canaanites; your father was an Amorite, and your mother a Hittite.

Ezekiel 16:45 You are the daughter of your mother, who loathed her husband and her children; and you are the sister of your sisters, who loathed their husbands and their children. Your mother was a Hittite and your father an Amorite.

THE AMORITES

Unlike many other Canaanite peoples, the Amorites are not anchored in a place called "Amor." Amorite is therefore a tribal-based name. Like the Canaanites under whose umbrella they fall, their name has both a wide and a narrow significance. "Amorites" is used to indicate the whole group of pre-Israelite inhabitants of Canaan (Genesis 15:16; 48:22; Joshua 10:12). In contrast, they also have rulers of their own (Genesis 14:7; Numbers 21:21-31). Three Amorites kings were Sihon, Og, and Mamre (Genesis 14:13; Numbers 32:33).

THE GIRGASHITES

Little is known about the Girgashites, save that they are regularly mentioned in the lists of pre-Israelite Canaan inhabitants. Some scholars identify them with a tribe in Phoenicia.[121] Some see connections between them and the "Garasenes" who lived around lake Genessaret (Matthew 8:26; Mark 5:1; Luke 8:26, 37; 5:1).[122]

THE HIVITES

The Hivites were a tribe (or tribes) located generally in Canaan, Lebanon and Syria. Hivites lived in central Palestine. The Scripture indicates that the lived in the area of Gibeon and Shechem (Genesis 34:2; Joshua 9:7; 11:19). In contrast, Second Samuel 24:6-7 first mentions Sidon, Tyre, and then the Hivites (north to south). This would place the Hivites well north into Lebanon and Syria (cf. Judges 3:3). On the basis of questionable arguments some scholars seek an explanation of the Hivite's identity by relating them both to the Horites (aboriginal people of Mt. Seir) and especially to the Hurrians (non-Hamites from the region south of the Caucasus Mountains). These associations should be rejected in favor of the explicit Biblical identification of the Hivites as Hamitic Black Canaanites.[123] Zibeon is called a Hivite in Genesis 36:2. Hamor the Hivite is called "the prince of the land" in Genesis 34:2. According to 1 Kings 9:20-21 Hivites served as workers for Solomon's building projects.

Five Phoenician Canaanite City-Dwellers

The first four of these Canaanite city-dwellers were situated on the Mediterranean coast in Phoenicia. The fifth was located somewhat inland. All these names can be identified with certainty.

THE ARKITES

The Arkites references the people who lived in Arqat. The modern town is Tell Arqah is located four miles from the Mediterranean and about 12 miles northeast of Tripoli, Syria. It was called "Caesarea Libani" (Caesarea in Lebanon) by the Romans. It is mentioned in 1 Chronicles 1:15.

THE SINITES

The Sinites are identified with the northern Phoenician city-state of Siyan(n)u. It was located at a large mound near the modern village of Siyanu in northern Lebanon. Some see "tenuous evidence" etymologically relating the Chinese to the Sinites.[124]

THE ARVADITES

The Arvadites are the people who dwelt in the island-city of Arvad in northern Syria. As the most northerly Phoenician city, it was located about 2.5 miles off the Mediterranean coast and about 30 miles north of Tripoli. According to the verses below, Arvadites served as rowers on Tyrian ships and as mercenaries near Tyre before its fall.

Ezekiel 27:8-11   {8} The inhabitants of Sidon and **Arvad** were your rowers; skilled men of Zemer were in you, they were your pilots. {9} The elders of Gebal and her skilled men were in you, caulking your seams; all the ships of the sea with their mariners were in you, to barter for your wares. {10} "Persia and Lud and Put were in your army as your men of war; they hung the shield and helmet in you; they gave you splendor. {11} The men of **Arvad** and Helech were upon your walls round about, and men of Gamad were in your towers; they hung their shields upon your walls round about; they made perfect your beauty.

THE ZEMARITES

South of Arvad we find the city of the Zemarites. In modern times the place is known as *Sumra*. The Zemarites settled on the Mediterranean coast near the mouth of the Eleutheros River. It is possible that the "Zemaraim" of Joshua 18:22 and 2 Chronicles 13:4 reference the Zemarites who migrated south.[125]

THE HAMATHITES

Finally, there are the Hamathites. The population of Hamath lived on the east bank of the Orontes, lying on one of the main trade-routes to the south from Asia Minor. Hamah, as it is called today, is 125 miles north of Damascus. The city is mentioned often in the Old Testament, being near the northern border of the promised land (e.g. Numbers 34:8; Joshua 13:5). According to

2 Kings 17:24ff. some of the Hamathites were settled in Samaria by the Assyrians. In David's day, Toi was the king of Hamath (2 Samuel 8:9ff; Tou in 1 Chronicles 18:9).

THE FAMILIES OF THE CANAANITES

The fourth Hamitic and second Canaanite "report" is provided in Genesis 10:18b-19. This report describes to us that "the families of the Canaanites" spread abroad, and then identifies the territorial boundaries of these peoples. What is clear about this description of Canaan – which encompasses the Phoenicians, the Philistines, and the cities of the plain – is that it reflects an Egyptian political hegemony in Asia. "Canaan is a general name for the Asian holdings of Egypt."[126]

3. Summary

The geopolitical dimension of the Canaanite genealogical line is evident. "Canaan" was the home of varied Hamitic ethnic entities. They were all known as "Canaanites" by virtue of the land in which they lived and their ethnic roots. From the outside they were viewed as a political whole from an Egyptian viewpoint. These indigenous people of Canaan were Black.

H.

How Can Ham be "Black" and

His Brothers not?

At this point a crucial question is raised. If Ham (and the nation which descended from him) was definitely "Black" or "Negroid," then why would not the other sons of Noah, Shem and Japheth, likewise be classified as "Black" or "Negroid?" Did not they come from the same parents, Noah and his wife?

This is a very interesting question, whose answer points in the direction for the "Black" origin of all humanity! The reasoning goes this way.

1. An Ethnological Table, Not Necessarily Racial

First, the three-fold division of the Table of Nations as given above should not be regarded as the three racial divisions of humanity, with the Semites being one, the Hamites being two, and the Japhethites being three. Rather than three comprehensive racial divisions of humanity, the three sons of Noah and the peoples who sprang from them are essentially nation-divisions or ethnic entities. The Table of Nations is more ethnological than anything else.[127]

2. Explicit Blackness in Shem's Line

Second, with such being the case, it is possible that "Blackness" is also present, not only within Ham's line, but also within the lines of the other sons. For example, one might refer to "Elam" who appears in the line of Shem (Genesis 10:21, 22). The Elamites, a people associated with the ancient Persians, are regarded by many scholars as a Black or Negroid people.[128] Thus, Blackness has surfaced (explicitly) in the line of Shem – a line which implicitly may contain a greater degree of Blackness than we are able to explicitly ascertain.

3. Humanity's Pre-Flood Make-Up

Third, thus, the pre-Flood make-up of humanity (prior to Genesis 10) was either: a) composed of a single original Black group, of which eight people remained following the Flood (cf. the Blackness of color of Adam, who was made from the dust of the ground, and therefore of Eve who originated by God from Adam); or b) composed of several racial/ethnic groups of which all were destroyed save eight people who all reflected a distinct Black line due to their common parentage (cf. also Genesis 11:1ff.).

Concerning the first possibility of the pre-Flood make-up of humanity – a single original Black group – we make reference to the January 11, 1988 *Newsweek* article entitled "The Search for Adam & Eve." The article, which is written from a statedly evolutionary concept of the origin of humanity,[129] pictures a Black Adam and Eve on the front cover which captures the thesis of the article as reflected in the findings of DNA researchers. This discovery may in fact be a confirmation that the original woman and man (Adam being her "father" through origination) as the first-fruits of humanity's creation, were indeed Black.[130]

Following are summary comments of several lines of thought taken from the *Newsweek* article. Keep in mind that the scientists dated their "Eve" (they hesitated at using the name) evolutionarily at about 200,000 years old.

The scientist presented their "Eve" as most likely a "dark-haired, black-skinned woman." They traced her through an international assortment of genes and followed a trail of DNA that led them to a single woman from whom they believe all people are descended. Their evidence indicated that "Eve" lived in "sub-Saharan Africa." Meanwhile, other geneticists are trying to trace humanity back to a scientifically derived Adam whom they accept as a commonly regarded "great father" of all people.

The researchers went on to say that the DNA of the babies tested appeared to form a family tree which was "rooted in Africa."

One category of this DNA data was found only in some babies of recent African descent. A second category was found in everyone else and the other African people. So they concluded that the DNA tree began in Africa, from which a group of Africans emigrated thus splitting off to form a second branch of DNA which they carried into the rest of the world. Regardless of which category, all the babies' DNA was traceable back, ultimately, to one woman.

Finally, the DNA scientists are still looking for that one person whom they may classify as an "Adam" – a man from whom we are all descended. They reason that since all humanity is descended from Eve's daughters, any common male ancestor of these daughters would be a common ancestor of all people living today. Such a common male ancestor would not necessarily be their "Eve's" husband. Perhaps she had more than one, the scientists speculate. Yet, all of "Eve's" daughters certainly had the same maternal grandfather. Therefore, the scientists conclude, the only safe reasoning points in the direction that "Adam was Eve's father."

It should be noted that this latter point is just, in fact, what the Bible teaches! The Biblical Adam was very much the "father" of Biblical Eve – in the sense that Eve originated from Adam. The woman's existence did not come about independently of the man. The Scripture says, "So the Lord God caused a deep sleep to fall upon the man , and while he slept took one of his ribs and closed up its place with flesh; and the rib which the Lord God had taken from the man he made into a woman and brought her to the man. Then the man said, 'This at last is bone of my bones and flesh of my flesh; she shall be called Woman, because she was taken out of Man'." (Genesis 2:21-23).

4. Blackness, Humanity's Norm

Fourth, therefore, the existence of whiteness and the development of "white" people occurred later in the history of humanity. In other words, the evidence – Biblical evidence, archaeological evidence, and DNA-wise evidence – points in the direction that Blackness is humanity's norm and whiteness is the exception rather than the rule, the derivation, not the origination.[131]

If Adam was from Africa, then all people are "African" in one sense, for all people are derived from, according to the Scripture, one common ancestor – Adam; God's Adam whose physicalness must have been gloriously colorful, for he was created in the image of God from the dust of the ground.[132]

Having stated the above, whose ideas are based in the findings of much research undertaken by competent scholars and scientists, we yet recognize that most persons would like a more immediate starting point for establishing the Black/African identity of Biblical persons and nations. So, at any rate, we say that Genesis 10 is one of the best starting points in the Scripture. Starting with the Hamitic line is quite useful.

I.

The Blackness of Original Humanity

and Prototypical Civilizations

As the preceding discussion demonstrates, there is a growing acceptance of the fact that humanity was Black and African from the outset. The information being gathered by archaeologists, ancient historians, and the like speaks the truth loud and clear that, to quote Cheikh Anta Diop,

> ...the whole human race had its origin, just as the ancients had guessed, at the foot of the Mountains of the Moon. Against all expectations and in defiance of recent hypotheses it was from *this place* that men moved out to people the rest of the world...of necessity the earliest men were ethnically homogeneous and negroid... [and] there were only two routes available by which these early men could move out to people the other continents, namely, the Sahara and the Nile valley.[133]

The traditional view teaches that humanity's origin is found, not in Egypt, Africa, but in Asia, in lower Mesopotamia in the area of the Tigris-Euphrates Valley, if in fact the two areas were not geographically distinct from one another in pre-historic time – a not improbable assumption.[134]   Though the verses in Genesis 2:8-14ff. explaining the geography of the Garden in Eden do appear to reference the Mesopotamian area,[135] it must be kept in mind that the names of the river headstreams – Pishon, Gihon, Tigris, and Euphrates – were names given to rivers thousands, if not millions, of years following God's creation of humanity and placing them in the Garden in Eden.   Moreover, people have often given identical names to different places or territories during different time-periods.[136]

Nevertheless, whether one accepts the latter view, that humanity began in Asia, or the more substantiated view, that humanity began in Egypt, Africa, there is a single thread that is common to both. Humanity at its outset was indeed "Black," a fact that is affirmed by the first civilizations which emerged. For Asia's lower Mesopotamian indigenous population was Black.[137] They were the Sumerian "Blackheads" dwelling in the land of Shinar.[138] "The first Mesopotamian civilizations were black."[139] The Sumerians were the "founders and guardians of West Asia's oldest known civilization."[140]

It is a noted fact that wherever ancient civilizations have emerged on the face of this earth, they were Black. Whether in Egypt, Cush, Sumer, Asia, North America or South America, each cultural center of the ancient world was "Hamitic in origin."[141] Blacks are the progenitors of humanity and the creative originators of culture and civilizations.[142]

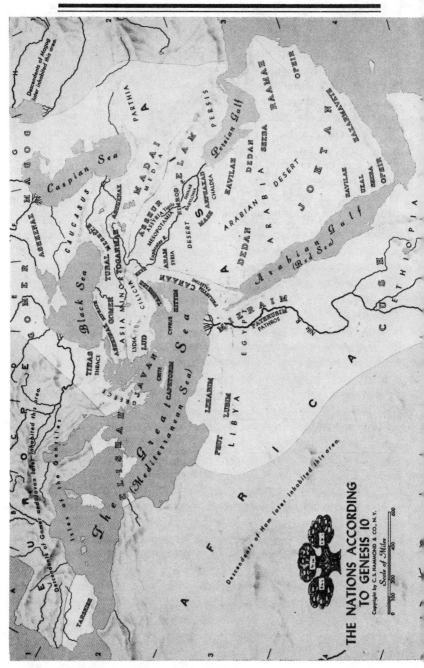

THE NATIONS ACCORDING
TO GENESIS 10

Copyright by C.S. HAMMOND & CO., N.Y.

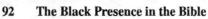

Scale of Miles

0   100   200   300   400   500   600

92   The Black Presence in the Bible

SECTION VI

Special Cushite Discussion

A. The Lands of the Cushite People

B. "Cush": An Ancient Identifying Term

of Black People

C. The Accurate Geographical Identification of

Cush in Contrast to Modern Ethiopia

D. The Reason for Consistently Reading "Cush"

in Our Minds When Reading the

King James Version.

A.

The Lands of the Cushite People

Cush/Ethiopia as used in the Scripture is not limited to defining a place or people limited to the African region south of Egypt. It is in fact an inter-continental designation of people living within both Asia and Africa. The African and Cushite presence was found in various places in the ancient world including such places as: Arabia, Elam-Persia, Mesopotamia, Greece, India, Phoenicia, Crete, and Canaan, not to mention Egypt and of course "Ethiopia" in Africa.

1. African-Cush, South of Egypt

In what place did the nation of Cush come to dwell? The ancient Cushites lived on the continent of Africa (though not exclusively there). When Cush is mentioned, most people familiar with geography immediately reference a part of Africa. From the perspective of the ancient Israelite people living in Canaan land (Palestine), Cush was a southernly country lying as far off as possible. Cush, to them, was the land of a people living on the edge of the southern horizon. According to the Biblical record, the Hebrew-Israelites, as they gazed south into Africa, knew of no other people living beyond the land of Cush.[143] The Bible, Egyptian records and the Greek historian Herodotus all work together to substantiate the geographical location of Cush on Africa's continent.[144] The geographical location of ancient Cush (known Biblically as either "Cush" or "Ethiopia") must be viewed in a distinct way apart from the geographical location of modern Ethiopia.

The kingdom of Cush, being located on Africa, was situated south of the territory of Egypt in the north Sudan. The Sudan is a region lying across Africa. It is south of the Sahara and north of the equator. Cush was located south of the kingdom of Egypt. Matter of fact, the ancient Egyptians used the term "Cush" in order to refer to their brothers immediately to their south. However, the term

"Cush" can be traced back to a self-designation of Cushite people which predates Egyptian usage.[145]

The Nile River is in East Africa. It flows north from Lake Victoria to the Mediterranean Sea. Along one branch it measures 3,473 miles, while on another branch it measures 4,175 miles. The Nile River has six cataracts, or steep rapids and waterfalls over granite rock formations protruding from the soil. They are located in the Nubian sandstone belt. The first one in the North is at Aswan, and the rest are counted southward to the sixth cataract. There are 700 miles between the first and the sixth cataract which is north of Khartum in the Sudan. There are also several minor cataracts in the Nile.[146]

We mentioned the above in order to say that around 2000 B.C. the kingdom of Cush was located between the second and third cataracts of the Nile River. Later, however, Cush was geographically located in a wider area. The term came to include all of what later became known as Nubia, the region lying across Africa, south of the Sahara and north of the equator. Still later, the designation "Cush" came to include Arabia, two areas separated merely by the Red Sea. It also grew to mean the southern extremity of Egypt, thus being identified with Upper Egypt. The city of Napata was the first capital of the Cushite kings. It was located in Sudan beyond the third cataract of the Nile River.

Bishop Dunston in *The Old Testament and Its World* noted that

The area of ancient Cush (Kush) lies almost due east of, and equally as southernly as Mauritania, which was the location of ancient Ghana that arose and flourished between 300 B.C. and 1200 A.D. And the area lies in the same relationship to ancient and modern Mali...[147]

Drusilla Dunjee Houston (1876-1941) wrote the *Wonderful Ethiopians of the Ancient Cushite Empire*. This book was outstanding when first published in 1926 and its value to our understanding of Cush is still very great today, as evidenced by its re-release in 1985. We learn much about the land of Cush from Houston's work.

The third chapter in *Wonderful Ethiopians* is entitled "Ancient Ethiopia, The Land." In this chapter Houston discusses 1) Ethiopia a Land Richer and Broader than Egypt; 2) Cushite Wealth Sprang from World-wide Trade;   3) The Gold Mines and Emeralds of Ethiopia;   and 4) The Infinite Number of Monuments and Temples.[148]

Some of Houston's research information on the land of Cush includes the following. The territory of Cush was also called the "land of the blacks" (Beled-es-Soudan, an Arab designation). The ancient kingdom of Meroe was Upper Nubian and was divided into agricultural and grazing lands.   At the height of its prosperity Meroe was established upon as broad an economic basis as Egypt or Mesopotamia. The people grew grains upon lands richer and wider than the whole of Egypt, with pastures of limitless plains.   Their lands were lands of heavy rains.   Precious stones were there in abundance.[149]

The early prosperity and greatness of Ethiopia sprang from its trade.   There was an intimate connection between Egypt and Ethiopia commercially. From Cush came gold, topaz,[150] emeralds, roses, vine olives, sugar cane and cotton. Orange and lemon trees grew to the size of apple trees.   Cush had an inexhaustible supply of building material of the first quality, including sandstone, limestone and granite.   It was a land of pyramids, temples, colonnades, avenues of animals and statues.[151]

In one of her concluding remarks Houston said,

> the natural products of Ethiopia, her commerce, the strength of her armies, spoken of by the Scriptures as a thousand thousand, we find them a substantial foundation for ancient traditions about that nation.[152]

Among these traditions are the testimony that the Cushites were "proud and mighty." This leads to our next section.

2. Cush All Over the Biblical World; Africa and Asia

Having described the popular understanding of the place where the Cushite people dwelt, that is, in Africa south of Egypt, we can now move to state what has not been so obvious for many of us. The truth is that the term "Cush" refers to other places (besides those south of Egypt) in Africa as well as in Asia. We gain this information from ancient writers, whose views should be accepted above the views of modern persons who did not see firsthand what the ancient persons saw and understood.

The appropriate question to ask ourselves at this point is, What are the different places to which the term "Cush" refers, and therefore which places were inhabited by these Black people to a greater or lesser degree? Is Bishop Dunston accurate when he states,

> Black people of the Old Testament world were not confined to Egypt and Cush, however. References have traced them to various parts of Asia, including the Caspian area and India, where Herodotus saw 'the same tint of skin, which approaches that of the Ethiopians'?[153]

Initially we refer to *Africa and Africans as Seen by Classical Writers,* by Hansberry.[154] The following summaries are taken from the first chapter entitled "Ancient Designations for Ethiopia." In this chapter Hansberry deals with Greek, Ethiopian, Egyptian, as well as Asian designations of Ethiopia (Cush).

First, citing the ancient geographer Ephorus, Hansberry sets the tone by stating that even though many contemporary students of history use the term "Ethiopians" in reference only to the people who lived south of Egypt, this limited use should not lead us to so circumscribe the usage of ancient persons. The territory designated "Ethiopia" varied from time to time. It was applied to lands and people living in both Africa and Asia. Modern discoveries and research have shown that in ancient times a black skinned people, "Aethiops," made up an essential dimension of the populations of Arabia, Mesopotamia, Persia and India. The information gained by Hansberry in his studies led him to use two different designations referring to Cush throughout his work. He used "Ethiopia" to refer to the territory which corresponds roughly to the Republic of the Sudan. At other times he used "Greater Ethiopia" to refer to the broader area of the Cushite lands just as Greeks used the term.[155]

In the *Wonderful Ethiopians of the Ancient Cushite Empire* Drusilla Dunjee Houston establishes the presence of ancient Cushites in places other than Africa south of Egypt. Her thrust is captured in the "Introductory Note" by W. Paul Coats. Coats shows how Houston establishes connections among the ancient Black populations of Arabia, Persia, Babylonia and India. She was drawn to the conclusion that the ancient Black people who dwelt in these geographic areas were "culturally linked" and had been the progenitors of civilizations in all these places.[156]

The same is affirmed of Houston's argument in the *Wonderful Ethiopians* "Afterword" by Asa G. Hilliard III. He cites Houston's perception that the ancient Cushite civilization spread through both the African continent as well as through the broader world. It spread in Arabia, Greece, Persia, and India. Signs of the name "Kush" as well as the people's culture and their actual physical presence could be found in these and other places. For example, Hindu Kush in India and also the Black Dravidian population dwelling there.[157]

We can trace the movement of Houston's thesis, which in fact is her studied understanding of the historical movement of Blacks. She identifies Blacks with the origin of civilization, focuses on the work of Blacks or 'Ethiops' in nation building – Cush being the name of the ancient African kingdom and civilization – shows how this ancient civilization spread throughout the continent of Africa impacting Egypt and spreading throughout the world at-large.[158]

John G. Jackson in his powerful little booklet, *Ethiopia and the Origin of Civilization* says

> In modern geography the name Ethiopia is confined to the country known as Abyssinia, an extensive territory in East Africa. In ancient times Ethiopia extended over vast domains in both Africa and Asia. 'It seems certain,' declares Sir E. A. Wallis Budge, 'that classical historians and geographers called the whole region from India to Egypt, both countries inclusive, by

the name of Ethiopia, and in consequence they regarded all the dark-skinned and black peoples who inhabited it as Ethiopians. Mention is made of Eastern and Western Ethiopians and it is probable that the Easterners were Asiatics and the Westerners Africans."[159]

We refer once again to the writings of Dr. Charles B. Copher in "The Black Man in the Biblical World." In this article he deals with the geographical divisions of the Biblical world which he describes as "**Egypt-African Cush; Asiatic Cush; and Mediterranean Lands.**"[160] Copher presents various lines of evidence which establish his thesis, while using the following sources as viewed from the perspective of the Hebrew-Israelite-[Judahite]-Jewish accounts, traditions and legends: the biblical Table of Nations, the Babylonian Talmud, and Midrashim.[161]

In a second article entitled "Blacks and Jews in Historical Interaction: The Biblical/African Experience," Dr. Copher continues his thesis by stating that he himself

assembled several categories of evidence that testify to a Black including Negro presence in the Biblical world. This Black presence was to be found in Egypt, African Cush, Asiatic Cush, and in eastern Mediterranean lands...The evidences testify that, according to American sociological definitions of Negro, the ancient Egyptians were Negroes; that according to modern anthropological and ethnological definitions the ancient Egyptian population included a large percentage of so-called Negroes, possibly 25% as an average across the long period of time that was ancient Egyptian history. **They indicate that the African Cushites (Ethiopians) were predominantly of Negroid identity; and that Blacks, including Negroes, during Biblical times, inhabited parts of Asia from the Indus River Valley westwards into Elam-Peria, Mesopotamia, and parts of Arabia, Phoenicia, Canaan, Crete and Greece.** Further, the evidence indicates that, *in the main*, wherever in the Bible Hamites are referred to there were peoples who today in the Western world would be classified as Black, and Negroid. Additionally, they establish a Black element within the ancient Hebrew-Israelite Jewish population itself."[162]

According to the preceding discussion, we are able to affirm several things. **First** we should educate ourselves to accept the perspective of ancient writers on their understanding of "Cush." They had greater access to firsthand information than we do. **Second**, the term "Cush" is not limited to identifying an African region south of Egypt, but is in fact an intercontinental designation including people living in Asia and Africa. **Third**, the African and Cushite presence was found in various places in the ancient world including such places as: Arabia, Elam-Persia, Mesopotamia, Greece, India, Phoenicia, Crete, and Canaan, not to mention Egypt and of course "Ethiopia" in Africa.

We have taken the time to discuss the places inhabited by the ancient Cushites for an important reason. We must first establish the presence of Black people in the world which gave us the Bible and secondly relate that Biblical world presence of Blacks to those Black persons, peoples and nations referred to in the Bible. This sound approach is subtly captured in the title of Copher's article mentioned above, "The Black Man in the Biblical World," as well as in the title of Dunston's work, *The Black Man in The Old Testament and Its World*.

B.

"Cush": An Ancient Identifying Term

of Black People

An ancient term which is used to identify Black people in the Bible is the word "Ethiopia" or "Cush," or one of their derivatives. These terms (each expressing the underlying identical Hebrew term) designate either a person, a people, or the land from which they come.

"Ethiopia" comes from a Greek word meaning "dark-faced" or "burnt-faced." Hansberry said that the term is distinctly European. African usage of the term in reference to themselves or their country followed the European usage. Neither did the ancient Egyptians nor the Hebrews use the term in reference to Africans.[163]

"Cush" is a more ancient term and comes from a Hebrew word meaning "black." The Hebrew word is a transliteration of an ancient Egyptian word used with reference to their brothers to their South, "Kush."

"Kush" reflects an indigenous Ethiopian term. It was a self-identification term. The Ethiopians designated a major part, if not all, of their land as "Kesh," identified with Egyptian "Kush" and the Hebrew word for "Cush." Hansberry noted that these designations of "Cush" were used of Ethiopia in Africa south of Egypt by the Egyptians and the peoples of Western Asia for thousands of years. To the Egyptians the term "Kush" signified an area roughly from "the headwaters of the Atbara and the Blue Nile eastward to the Indian Ocean, the Arabian Gulf, and the southern reaches of the Red Sea."[164]

At one time it was thought that "Kush" and words derived from this term originated in Egypt. However, discoveries now reveal that "Kush" was indigenous to the country and peoples to which the term was applied. It was not until the second millenium B.C. that "Kush" appeared in Egyptian writings. In the Egyptian New Empire period, "Kush" became one of the most familiar and widely used terms in Egyptian geographical and historical literature.[165]

Depending on which translation of the Scripture is being used, the reader can easily trace either of the terms "Cush" or "Ethiopia" through the pages of the Bible. Either appears in many different Scriptural passages, especially within the Old Testament. In addition to Cush/Ethiopia, there are other words and terms which, when studied, indicate a reference to Black people. However, none of them are as renowned as Cush/Ethiopia.

A survey of the Authorized Version (and some modern translations) will reveal to the reader that the translators did not use either "Ethiopia" or "Cush" consistently throughout, even though this

would have been desired.[166] For either term (as used in the Old
Testament) reflects one and the same Hebrew word, and indicates
the Black ethnic make-up and roots of the bearer. At times, Cush
designates different geographical places besides Cush/Ethiopia
south of Egypt, Africa, a territory occupied by an indigenous
African people. Therefore, the reader of the Scripture should fix his
mind to see the identicalness of "Cush" and "Ethiopia" – referencing
a person or people of common Black African heritage – each time
either term comes across the Biblical written page.

C.

The Accurate Geographical Identification of

Cush in Contrast to Modern Ethiopia

Most people know about the African nation known as Ethiopia.
Thus far, we have learned that in Bible translations of especially the
Old Testament, the words "Ethiopia" and "Cush" are synonymous,
though some Bible translations do not use either term consistently.
At this point, what we need to know is this: When the Bible reads
"Ethiopia"/"Cush" is it saying something about the African nation
known to us contemporarily as Ethiopia?

The answer to this question is most often "No." When the Bible
reads "Cush/Ethiopia" it is not referring exclusively or primarily to
the modern nation of Ethiopia, though the name "Ethiopia" is the
same.

The modern Ethiopia is an independent country occupying some
450,000 square miles in eastern Africa between the Sudan (on its
west and northwest) and Somalia on its east and southeast. The
Red Sea is on its northeast, and Kenya is on its southwest. Its
population is about 27 million. It was formerly known as Abyssinia.

The people of modern Ethiopia claim descent from the ancient kingdom of Saba, which we know as South Arabia, and do not regard themselves as a wholly African people. Their ethnic composition is extremely diverse, as a result of racial and linguistic integration which began in ancient times. Their culture is characterized as "Sabaean-African."[167]

As stated above, Biblical Ethiopia, as used in most references, was also located on the continent of Africa but was situated south of the territory of Egypt in the north Sudan.

Having made a comparison/contrast of the primary geographical location of Cush/Biblical Ethiopia to modern Ethiopia we should now restate the important point made above. Cush/Ethiopia as used in the Scripture is not limited to defining a place or people limited to the African region south of Egypt. It is in fact an inter-continental designation including in its scope people living in Asia and Africa. The African and Cushite presence was found in various places in the ancient world including such places as: Arabia, Elam-Persia, Mesopotamia, Greece, India, Phoenicia, Crete, and Canaan, not to mention Egypt and of course "Ethiopia" (Cush) in Africa.[168]

D.

The Reason for Consistently Reading "Cush" in Our Minds When Reading the King James Version

We know that in the Bible, particularly speaking of the King James Version, "Ethiopia" is synonymous with "Cush." We also know that when the Bible mentions either of these terms that most often it is referring to a geographical area of Africa called the Sudan, which is located south of Egypt, and to the people who dwelt there. It is not primarily referring to the area which we now know as modern Ethiopia, or Abyssinia, located on the eastern coast of Africa, though the Biblical designation did at times encompass this area.

At this point a critical question may be raised: Why didn't the Bible translators of the *Authorized Version* (*KJV*) simply and consistently use the more accurate term "Cush" to describe this land and its people?

The answer to this question can be approached from at least two perspectives which are interrelated. Initially, let us be cognizant that in each translation of the Bible, whatever version, there is always a measure of interpretation present. This can't be avoided, but only minimized to a degree.

It is the nature of Bible translations to attempt to make the Word of God clear to the intended readers. So the translator(s) reads the original languages in which the Bible was written (Hebrew in the Old Testament and Greek in the New Testament) and translates these languages into the language of the reader. In our case, the Scripture is translated into English. However, an exact word for word translation is impossible, if not cumbersome. Therefore the translator tries to get into the meaning of what is written, and thereby seeks to convey this meaning to his readers. In many cases this process makes for the intelligent and smooth reading of a particular version. But this process of translation also allows the translator's opinions (interpretation) to ease into the translation, whether for good or for bad.[169]

Therefore, depending on the particular translator(s) we will find that if he (they) thought a given passage would be better understood by use of the word "Ethiopia" rather than "Cush," then he (they) would use the former term instead of the latter. This is done even though the underlying word in the Hebrew language of the Bible is the same throughout. This process can be observed in different versions and their marginal notes, including the *King James Version*, the *Revised Standard Version*, and the *Septuagint* (the Greek translation of the Hebrew Old Testament).[170]

Then there is a second reason for the inconsistent use of words by translators in their translations of Scripture. This reason is most disturbing. It stands to reason that if there is some unavoidable interpretation present within each translation, that there could also be present within each translation some interpretation that was intentional, even intentionally misleading. This, we would suggest to you, is the second reason for the inconsistent handling of "Cush/Ethiopia" in some versions of the Bible.

In this regard all readers of the King James Version must give considerable thought to the argument presented by Bishop Dunston concerning this point as it relates to the use of "Ethiopia" and "Cush." Let me encapsulate his argument.

Dunston puts forth good historical evidence that 17th century England was familiar with the Black man from south Sahara Africa. The people of this geographical area of the Sudan were called "Cush" by the ancient Egyptians and the Hebrews. They were called "Ethiopians" by the Greeks, "Nubians" by the Christians in the 6th century A.D., "Bildad as Sudan" (the land of the Blacks) by the Arab Muslims in 700 A.D., and "Negroes" by later Europeans.

The Black presence was part of the English and colonial scene, but these people were not called "Ethiopians" but "Negroes." Nevertheless, even though the King James translators (who wrote their translation in 1611) were aware of the geographical homeland of these Black people in the Bible, they still called them "Ethiopians." For the term "Ethiopia" did not image a Black man to the English reading white mind, but it imaged a "white man in blackish color" due to the hair texture, skin color, Arabian heritage, and geographical location of the modern Ethiopian people. Furthermore, the King James translators chose the rendering of "Ethiopia" despite making other significant endeavors toward making the Scripture plain to their English readers. For example, they used the term "Dukes" in reference to the sons of Esau because the term highlighted the royal place and prerogatives of Esau's sons even though the culture of the Hebrews knew nothing of "Dukes."[171]

Why? Simply because the King James translators refused to identify the Black people whom they held as slaves with the Black people written about in the Bible. They were motivated by racism, the need to justify slavery and pacify their consciences, and for other socioeconomic considerations. The translators could have identified the Biblical people of Cush by their "Black" color as the Greeks had done.[172] They could have written the ancient and great "Cush." On the other hand, and at the opposite extreme, their point could also have been made by using the despicable term "nigger" in their Biblical translation – 17th century England would have immediately been able to identify these Biblical people! Instead, they chose to write otherwise and inconsistently. In so doing, they have misled millions of Bible readers for well over three centuries. So goes the argument of Bishop Dunston.

Being faced with, to cite Dunston, such a grave mis-identification and "disservice to the Christian Church in general, and to the Black African and his descendants in particular,"[173] what should be our response? Each time the serious student of the Bible reads the *Authorized Version* (*King James Version*) and observes the word "Ethiopia" therein, he should educate his mind to think "Cush." And Cush means "Black African." Most of these people inhabited the Sudan, and others were found in a number of other geographical areas of the Biblical world. Their "roots" were indeed Black African. This identification is what the Hebrew language says, and this is what the Scripture means in all truth. Any other translation or understanding of the Hebrew word underlying "Cush/Ethiopia" falls short of "rightly handling the word of truth" (cf. 2 Timothy 2:15).

SECTION VII

Non-Hamitic Peoples
Descendants of Japheth and Shem

A. Japheth and His Descendants the "Japhethites"

B. Shem and His Descendants the "Semites"

Non-Hamitic Peoples

When studying the Black presence in the Bible, traced primarily through the descendants of Ham, invariably questions will arise concerning the identity and posterity of Noah's two other sons: Shem and Japheth. After all, these peoples do comprise two other major ethnic branches of humanity.

Who are the descendants of Shem and Japheth? Though the people of Shem and Japheth do not fall within the mainstream of our subject, a glimpse at their family lines as presented in *Genesis 10* will serve to keep our study in focus.

A.

Japheth and His Descendants the "Japhethites"

Genesis 10:2-5

{2} The sons of Japheth: Gomer, Magog, Madai, Javan, Tubal, Meshech, and Tiras. {3} The sons of Gomer: Ashkenaz, Riphath, and Togarmah. {4} The sons of Javan: Elishah, Tarshish, Kittim, and Dodanim. {5} From these the coastland peoples spread. These are the sons of Japheth in their lands, each with his own language, by their families, in their nations.

Japheth was the third son of Noah, though some think he was the second (cf. Genesis 10:21).[174] Japheth became the father of a wide-ranging family of peoples who came to settle to the north and, for the most part, to the west of the land of Palestine. They occupied an area all the way from Tarshish (Spain) on the West to the Caspian Sea on the East. Today these areas include the grass covered plains of southern Russia, much of Asia Minor, the islands of the Mediterranean, and the coasts of southern Europe. "Thus it appears that the descendants of Japheth were people who in the 2nd millennium were found in the regions to the N and NW of the Near East."[175]

Japheth's descendants included Gomer, Magog, Madai, Javan, Tubal, Meshech, and Tiras (Genesis 10:2). These people are the ancestors of the Indo-European (Caucasian) peoples.

The descendants of Gomer are believed to be the Gimirrai (or Gimirraya) of Assyrian records, a people known to the Greeks as Cimmerians. Magog is thought to be the father of the Scythians, and Madai the father of the Medes. The descendants of Javan are the Greeks, the Ionians cited in Homer, and particularly the Ionians who lived along the coast of western Asia Minor and the islands of the Aegean Sea. Tubal and Meshech are the progenitors of peoples of eastern Turkey, while the Tiras are the ancestors of the Tyresenoi of the Aegean islands, perhaps the Etruscans.

B.

Shem and His Descendants the "Semites"

Genesis 10:21-31

{21} To Shem also, the father of all the children of Eber, the elder brother of Japheth, children were born. {22} The sons of Shem: Elam, Asshur, Arpachshad, Lud, and Aram. {23} The sons of Aram: Uz, Hul, Gether, and Mash. {24} Arpachshad became the father of Shelah; and Shelah became the father of Eber. {25} To Eber were born two sons: the name of the one was Peleg, for in his days the earth was divided, and his brother's name was Joktan. {26} Joktan became the father of Almodad, Sheleph, Hazarmaveth, Jerah, {27} Hadoram, Uzal, Diklah, {28} Obal, Abimael, Sheba, {29} Ophir, Havilah, and Jobab; all these were the sons of Joktan. {30} The territory in which they lived extended from Mesha in the direction of Sephar to the hill country of the east. {31} These are the sons of Shem, by their families, their languages, their lands, and their nations.

Shem was the oldest son of Noah (Genesis 5:32, 1 Chronicles 1:4). He is the ancestor of the people known as Semites, though not all of his people spoke Semitic languages and dialects. The Messiah is directly related to him through his son Arpachshad (Genesis 11:10; Luke 3:36).

The descendants of Shem include Elam, Asshur, Arpachshad, Lud[176] and Aram[177] (Genesis 10:21-31). These peoples are geographically connected with the lands of Persia, Assyria, Chaldea, Lydia and Syria respectively. "These names suggest that the general area settled by the group stretched from Syria in the North through Mesopotamia to Arabia."[178] Some writers identify Arpachshad with the foothills of Armenia. The other sons of Shem, Uz, Hul, Gether, and Meshech, as listed in a parallel passage, 1 Chronicles 1:17, are identified as sons of Aram, the son of Shem. The verse in Chronicles may just be a general reference to the descendants of Shem.

The earliest home of the Semites is thought to have been in the foothills and valleys of Armenia. They migrated from this point into other areas where it has been established they settled. It is believed that Arpachshad remained the longest in his original settlement area. Eventually his people went southward and then westward to the plain of Shinar. Some think that the Semites had earlier contact with Egypt, and carried cultural affinities from there into Sumeria.

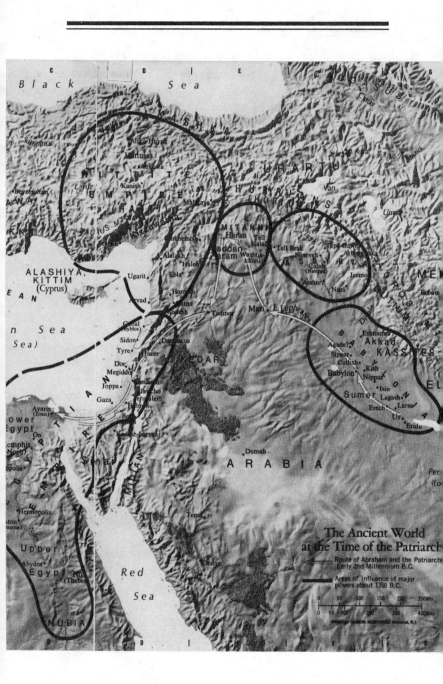

The Ancient World
at the Time of the Patriarch

— Route of Abraham and the Patriarch
Early 2nd Millennium B.C.

▬ Areas of influence of major
powers about 1350 B.C.

SECTION VIII

Black People in Their
Contemporary Biblical Setting

A. The Black World Surrounding Biblical History

B. An Old Testament Time Line:

"Black/Biblical/Historical/Geographical"

C. Explicit Black New Testament Persons

and Nations

A.

The Black World Surrounding Biblical History

As has been stated above, many Black nations contextualized the Biblical world. Dr. Charles Copher has demonstrated that the Biblical world is divided into three geographical areas: Egypt-African Cush; Asiatic Cush; and Mediterranean Lands.[179] Black people were to be found in Arabia, Elam-Peria, Mesopotamia, Greece, India, Phoenicia, Crete, Egypt, and Ethiopia.

It helps the student of Scripture to gain a perspective of the nations which impacted the Covenant community over the centuries, and the times in which they exerted their greatest influence. The following listing seeks to present such a chronological picture. The nations listed are those which during a particular time-period exercised a significant influence or domination over the affairs of the Covenant community.

Influence and Domination of Nations on the Hebrew-Israelite-Judahite-Jewish Covenant Community

Mesopotamia (2100-1200 +)[180] & Egyptians (2100-1200)

Judges (1200-1000)[181]

[United Monarchy of Israel (1000-850)]

Aramaeans (called Syrians) (850-800)

[Independence of Israel & Judah (800-745)]

Assyrians (732-609)

Egyptians (609-605)

Chaldeans (605-538)

Persians (538-332)

Greeks (332-165)

Maccabeans (165-63)

Romans (63 B.C.- A.D. +)

B.

An Old Testament Time Line

"Black/Biblical/Historical/Geographical"

When studying the Black presence in the Bible it is important for the student to gain a chronological perspective of the subject. The events of Scripture took place over the periods of hundreds of years. The Black personages and nations recorded in the Bible appeared at various points along this time span. Gaining a knowledge of these Black people in their historical and cultural context serves to further enlighten the student's understanding and appreciation of the subject.

Following are a number of time-periods in which Black Biblical people can be located. Below each period we list several Black individuals and or peoples who lived during the time. In the absence of a substantive Biblical exposition on each of these individuals, let us recall our definition of "Blackness." We use Black with reference to 1) actual "Black" skin color; 2) so-called "Negroid" characteristics; and 3) ancestral "Black blood."[182] A careful study of the Scripture will demonstrate that each of the individuals and or people listed are verifiably Black based on our definition.

1. The Patriarchal Period / 2000 - 1400 B.C.
   A. The Pharaoh of Genesis 12:15-20
   B. Melchizedek, Genesis 14:18ff.
   C. Hagar and Ishmael the son of Abraham, Genesis 16:1ff.
   D. Asenath, the wife of Joseph, Genesis 41:45ff.

2. The Enslavement-Exodus Period / 1400 - 1200 B.C.
   A. Jethro, the Midianite, Exodus 3:1
   B. The "Mixed-Multitude," Exodus 12:38
   C. The Cushite Wife of Moses, Numbers 12:1
   D. Phinehas, the grandson of Aaron, Numbers 25:7

3. The Judges Period / 1200 - 1000 B.C.
   A. Rahab, the harlot, Joshua 2:1
   B. Cushan-Rishathaim, Mesopotamian King, Judges 3:8
   C. Abimelech, son of Gideon, Judges 8:31
   D. Jephthah, the son of a prostitute, Judges 11:1

4. The United Monarchy Period / 1000 - 922 B.C.
   A. Uriah the Hittite, 2 Samuel 11:3
   B. Ha-Cushi, David's Messenger, 2 Samuel 18:21
   C. Pharaoh's daughter, Solomon's wife, 1 Kings 3:1
   D. The Queen of Sheba, 1 Kings 10:1ff.

5. The Divided Kingdom Period / 922 - 722 B.C.
   A. Zerah, the Ethiopian, 2 Chronicles 14:9-15; 16:8
   B. Shishak, Libyan king of Egypt, 1 Kings 14:25
   C. Jezebel, daughter of Ethbaal, 1 Kings 16:31-33
   D. The "Children of the Ethiopians," Amos 9:7

6. The Judah Kingdom Period / 721 - 586 B.C.
   A. Jehudi, Nethaniah, Shelemiah, Cushi, Jeremiah 36:14
   B. Ebedmelech, the Ethiopian, Jeremiah 38:7-13
   C. Tirhakah, a Pharaoh; Ethiopian Dynasty, 2 Kings 19:9
   D. Zephaniah, the son of Cushi, Zephaniah 1:1

7. The Exilic Period / 585 - 536 B.C.
   A. "By the waters of Babylon," Psalm 137:1ff.
   B. "Unto Ethiopia," Esther 1:1
   C. Tahpanhes, "The Palace of the Nubian," in Egypt, Jeremiah 43:7

8. The Restoration Period / 535 - N.T.
   A. Phinehas, father of a priest Eleazar, Ezra 8:33
   B. Geshem, of Kedar in Arabia, Nehemiah 2:19; 6:1-2, 6

C.

Explicit Black New Testament

Persons and Nations

The Old Testament contains many more references to Black people than the New Testament, even though each of the Testaments demonstrates a great interest in the varied ethnological divisions of humanity. Following are a few of the Black persons mentioned in the New Testament.

1. Explicit Black Persons Mentioned in Both Testaments

A. The Queen of the South, 1 Kings 10:1-10; Luke 11:31
B. Rahab the Harlot, Joshua 2:1-21; 6:22-25; Hebrews 11:31; James 2:25
C. Hagar, Genesis 16:1ff.; Galatians 4:21ff.
D. Melchizedek, Psalm 110:4; Hebrews 5:5ff.
E. The Sons of Joseph, Genesis 48; 47:31; Hebrews 11:21
F. The Haven of Egypt, Exodus 4:2; Hosea 11:1; Matthew 2:13-23

2. Explicit Black Persons Mentioned in the New Testament

A. The Wise Men, Matthew 2:1-12
B. Simon of Cyrene, Mark 15:21
C. Alexander & Rufus, Mark 15:21
D. The Canaanite Woman, Matthew 15:21-28; Mark 7:24-30
E. The Man of Ethiopia, Acts 8:26-40
F. Candace, Queen of the Ethiopians, Acts 8:27
G. Simeon called Niger, Acts 13:1-3
H. Lucius of Cyrene, Acts 13:1-3

3. Black Nations Represented at Pentecost

When the Christian Church was given birth by the Holy Spirit of God from heaven, Black persons were present. When the student of Scripture uncovers the identity of the various ethnic-groups who were visiting Jerusalem and consequently experienced this great outpouring of God, he begans to see by implication the Blackness of many of them.

We read in Acts 2:7-11:

"And they were amazed and wondered, saying, 'Are not all these who are speaking Galileans? And how is it that we hear, each of us in his own native language? Parthians and Medes and Elamites and residents of Mesopotamia, Judea and Cappadocia, Pontus and Asia, Phrygia and Pamphilia, Egypt and the parts of Libya belonging to Cyrene, and visitors from Rome, both Jews and proselytes, Cretans and Arabians, we hear them telling in our own tongues the mighty works of God'."

Just to mention several of the Black groups: there were the **Elamites**, the **Egyptians**, and the **Libyans belonging to Cyrene**.

What happened at Pentecost among these nations, a number of which are to be classified as Black, was a fulfillment of the prophecy recorded in Zephaniah 3:9-10:

"Yea, at that time I will change the speech of the peoples to a pure speech, that all of them may call on the name of the Lord and serve him with one accord. From beyond the rivers of Ethiopia my suppliants, the daughter of my dispersed ones, shall bring my offering."

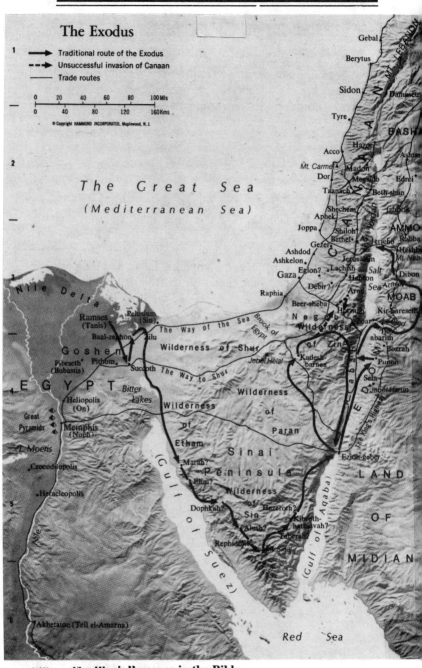

The Exodus

- ➤ Traditional route of the Exodus
- ➤ Unsuccessful invasion of Canaan
- —— Trade routes

0   20   40   60   80   100 Mis
0   40   80   120   160 Kms
© Copyright HAMMOND INCORPORATED, Maplewood, N.J.

The Great Sea
(Mediterranean Sea)

Gebal
Berytus
Sidon
Damascus
Tyre
BASHA
Acco
Hazor
Mt. Carmel
Ashtar
Dor
Madon
Megiddo
Edrei
Taanach
Beth-shan
Shechem
Jabbok
Aphek
AMMO
Joppa
Shiloh
Bethel
Jericho
Rabba
Gezer
Heshb
Ashdod
Jerusalem
Mt. Neb
Ashkelon
Lachish
Salt
Gaza
Eglon?
Hebron
Dibon
Raphia
Debir?
Sea
Arad
MOAB
Beer-sheba
Hormah
Kir-hareseth
Negeb
Zoar
Wilderness
abarim
Bozrah
Nile Delta
Ramses (Tanis)
Pelusium (Sin)
The Way of the Sea
Brook of Egypt
Wilderness of Zin
Punon
Baal-zephon
Zilu
Kadesh-barnea
Goshen
Pithom
Wilderness of Shur
Jebel Helal
Sela
Pibeseth (Bubastis)
Succoth   The Way to Shur
Jebel Harun
EGYPT
Heliopolis (On)
Bitter Lakes
Wilderness
Wilderness
Great Pyramids
Memphis (Noph)
of
of
L. Moeris
Etham
Sinai
Paran
Crocodilopolis
Marah?
Peninsula
Ezion-geber
Heracleopolis
Elim?
Wilderness
LAND
Dophkah?
of
Hazeroth?
Sin
Alush?
Kibroth-hattaavah?
OF
Taberah?
Rephidim
Mt. Sinai
MIDIAN
Akhetaton (Tell el-Amarna)
Red   Sea

Nile

(Gulf of Suez)

(Gulf of Aqaba)

The King's Highway

SECTION IX

The Blackness of the Old Covenant Community

A. The Blackness of the

   Hebrew-Israelite-Judahite-Jewish People

B. The Black Ancestry of Christ Jesus the Lord

C. Summary

The Blackness of the Old Covenant Community

One of the more enlightening aspects of the study of the Black presence in the Bible has to do with the ethnological make-up of the Old Covenant community. Here we are speaking of the Blackness, whether implicit or explicit, of the Hebrew-Israelite-Judahite-Jewish people spanning the centuries from Abraham, the father of the Hebrew people with whom God entered into Covenant, down to Christ Jesus Himself, the promised Messiah of God.

It is indeed possible for us to demonstrate 1) the Blackness of the Covenant-Messianic community; 2) the Blackness of the Messianic genealogical line; and 3) the Blackness of the Messiah Himself, Christ Jesus the Lord.

"Some maintain that there was a very pronounced presence of blacks, even Negroes, in the biblical world, including the ancient Hebrews-Israelites-[Judahites]-Jews," wrote Dr. Charles Copher.[183]

A.

The Blackness of the

Hebrew-Israelite-Judahite-Jewish People

1. The Covenant-Messianic Community

The evidence that Abraham, the father of the Biblical Hebrew people, though listed genealogically in the Table of Nations as a descendant of Shem, was Black may be demonstrated from a discussion about his place of origination, Ur of the Chaldees. "Chaldea" was located in South Babylonia. The name was used later to denote Babylonia as a whole, especially during the final dynasty of Babylonia (626-539 B.C.). The Chaldeans were a semi-nomadic tribe occupying the deserts between North Arabia and the Persian Gulf (cf. Job 1:17) who at a very early time settled in this area occupying Ur 'of the Chaldees' (cf. Genesis 11:28; Acts 7:4). They were distinct from the Aramaeans.[184]

Chaldea was "a land occupied by Cushites."[185] And it must be noted that the culture and civilization of this area are traceable back to Nimrod the son of Cush, according to Genesis 10:8-10. Sumer was the home of an indigenous people who called themselves "the Blackheads." It has been demonstrated that this indigenous Black people migrated into Sumer from the Nile Valley. Their Blackness and Africanness is attested in archaeological evidence, whose skulls contained the same variations of Ethiopic or Africoid skulls found in Africa's interior and in Egypt.[186]

Ur was probably the most powerful Sumerian city of its era. It was a flourishing city and dominated South Babylonia. Abraham, who may be dated around 2000 B.C., probably left the city at the height of its commercial prosperity.

Among the nations in which Abraham lived during his sojourn we find the Canaanites (Genesis 12:6), the Perizzites (13:7), the Philistines (21:34), the Egyptians (12:10), and the Hittites (Genesis 23). It is clear from Genesis 14:14, 15 that Abraham's household included servants who were not home-born. They probably were Egyptians who became a part of his group while he dwelt in Egypt, as did Hagar.

Then, we could speak of the descendants of Jacob, Israelites, who dwelt in the land of Goshen, Egypt. Joseph had become the forerunner for the family, and he had married the Egyptian Asenath, the daughter of Potiphera, priest of the city of On or Heliopolis. From this union two children were born, Ephraim and Manasseh (cf. Genesis 41:45, 50-52). These sons of Joseph became ancestors of the tribes of Israel bearing their names; two explicitly Black tribes.

The sojourn of the Israelites in Egypt saw them intermarrying with the native Egyptians. This accounts for the nation's tremendous growth during their 400 + year Egyptian stay. If there were 140 persons who made the trek with Jacob from Canaan into

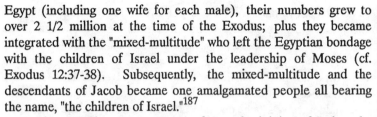

Egypt (including one wife for each male), their numbers grew to over 2 1/2 million at the time of the Exodus; plus they became integrated with the "mixed-multitude" who left the Egyptian bondage with the children of Israel under the leadership of Moses (cf. Exodus 12:37-38). Subsequently, the mixed-multitude and the descendants of Jacob became one amalgamated people all bearing the name, "the children of Israel."[187]

In the meantime, one must not forget the joining of Jethro the Midianite's family with the liberated Israelites. The Midianites were descendants of Abraham and Keturah, and were Cushites (cf. Genesis 25:1-4; Habakkuk 3:7 and Numbers 12:1). Moses married Zipporah "the Cushite," and their sons were Gershom and Eliezer (Exodus 18:1-3).

Over in the land of Canaan, a land already occupied by a Hamitic Black people, we find the Israelite people under Joshua's leadership of conquest, inter-marrying and forming alliances with the indigenous population. In Judges 3:1-6 we find that in Canaan dwelt the Philistines, the Canaanites, the Sidonians, the Hivites, the Hittites, the Amorites, the Perizzites, the Hivites, and the Jebusites. The Israelites inter-married with them and practiced their religion alongside the religion of their Hebrew-Israelite-Egyptian forefathers (cf. Joshua 24:14-15; Ezekiel 16:1-4, 44-45).

2. The Messianic Line

The genealogical line through which the Jewish Messiah was to come was ethnologically Black. This is demonstrable through the implicit Blackness as well as through specific Black persons who appeared in this line. The Messiah was to come through the line of Judah (Genesis 49:8-12).

Judah married Canaanite wives. One of these wives was named Bathshua and the other Tamar.[188] Both these wives were Canaanite (Genesis 38:7ff; 1 Chronicles 2:3, 4). The Messianic line continued through Tamar by a son named Perez. According to 1 Chronicles 2:1ff. we gain a picture of Judah's descendants through Tamar. One son of Judah through Tamar was **"Perez"** (v. 4), who was the father of **"Hezron"** (v. 5), who was the father of **"Ram"** (v. 9), who was the father of **"Amminadab,"** who was the father of **"Nahshon"** (v. 10), who was the father of **"Salma,"** who was the father of **"Boaz"** (v. 11), who was the father of **"Obed,"** who was the father of **"Jesse"** (v. 12), who was the father of **"David"** (v. 15).

Thus, the family tree of David back up to Judah was affected by explicitly Black Tamar the Canaanite. From this point the Davidic line can be traced through his lineal descendants Solomon, Rehoboam, Abijah, Asa, Jehoshaphat, Joram, Uzziah, Jotham, Ahaz, Hezekiah, Manasseh, Amon, Josiah, and Jechoniah (Matthew 1:6-11). From this point, which is the time of the Babylonian exile, the line of David continues right through to "Joseph the husband of Mary, of whom Jesus was born, who is called Christ" (Matthew 1:16).

According to Zephaniah 1:1, the "Hezekiah" mentioned above was the great-great-grandfather of the prophet Zephaniah. This is important information because this Hezekiah was the fourteenth king of the southern kingdom of Judah, the kingdom through which the Messianic line continued. Zephaniah says his father was named "Cushi," "son of Gedaliah, son of Amariah, son of Hezekiah" (1:1). Thus, the Messianic line proceeding from Hezekiah contained a pronounced degree of Blackness, demonstrated in the Cushite ethnicity of Zephaniah's father.

B.

The Black Ancestry of Christ Jesus the Lord

That Jesus Christ had Black ancestors, that is, people of Hamitic origin in His family line, can be demonstrated quite simply.

The genealogical information about Jesus Christ is provided us in two Gospels: Matthew 1:1-16 and Luke 3:23-38. These genealogical tables are reliable, providing detailed information about the Lord's ancestry.

There are basically two views held by Biblical scholars concerning these genealogical tables. One view has it that the genealogical table in Matthew gives Joseph's family tree and that the one in Luke gives Mary's family tree. The other view has it that the genealogical information in both Gospels gives only Joseph's line. As such, Matthew's information provides the line of official succession to the Davidic throne, and Luke's information gives details of the actual physical ancestors of Joseph back to David.

Whichever view of the Gospel's information is accepted, it will become evident that both genealogical tables have a significant bearing on the fact that Christ Jesus had Black/African, that is, Hamitic ancestors. Before we give the simple details, let us first establish the ancient family tree of Black people as recorded in the Scriptures.

It is acceptable by both biblical and non-biblical scholars that Hamitic peoples (descendants of Noah's son Ham) are the ancestors and originators of an explicit line of Black/African peoples all over the earth. Ham became the father of Cush, Egypt, Put and Canaan–all Black descendants of their Black father.

At this point we are now in a position to further appreciate the Black ancestry of Christ. This information is anchored in the genealogical table of Matthew, and, in this particular approach, and to the surprise of some, it concerns no less that three of the four women who are noted as being ancestors of the Lord!

The first woman is mentioned in Matthew 1:3 and is named Tamar. The story of Tamar can be found in Genesis 38. Tamar was known to be a Canaanite woman by virtue of her implied identification as a Canaanitess,[189] and where she dwelt, in a city called Timnath. Timnath was in the vicinity of Adullam, a known Canaanite town (cf. 38:1, 2, 6, 11, 13). Tamar became an ancestor of Christ Jesus through a child she mothered by her own father-in-law Judah. The child's name was Perez (Matthew 1:3).

The second woman is mentioned in Matthew 1:5 and is named Rahab. The story of Rahab is found in Joshua 2:1-21 and 6:17-25. Rahab was known to be a Canaanite, an inhabitant of the city of Jericho. She was the prostitute who helped the two Israelite spies when they surveyed the land of Canaan. As a result of her actions of faith, the lives of Rahab and her household were spared during the Israelite conquest of Jericho (cf. Hebrews 11:31; James 2:25). It was an ancestor of Christ Jesus named Boaz who was in fact the son of Rahab the Canaanite (Matthew 1:5).

The third woman who was a Black ancestor of Christ Jesus is mentioned in Matthew 1:6 as the "wife of Uriah," Bathsheba by name. The story of Bathsheba is recorded in 2 Samuel 11. Most know the story of "David and Bathsheba." What is often overlooked is the fact that Bathsheba was married to Uriah the Hittite. It is widely known and accepted that the Hittites were a Hamitic people. They descended from Heth, a son of Canaan (Genesis 10:15; 23:10).[190] If in fact Bathsheba shared the same ethnic origin as her husband (a not improbable assumption), then the child born to her and David, Solomon by name, did indeed have Black ancestry in his veins. Solomon was an ancestor of Christ Jesus (Matthew 1:6).

Immediately the objection may be raised: But Joseph, whose genealogy is recorded in Matthew's Gospel, had nothing to do with the birth of Jesus, for Jesus was miraculously conceived and born to a woman who was a virgin.[191] Joseph's seed had nothing to do with the humanity of Jesus. Thus, any reference to Black African blood in the genealogical line of Jesus through Joseph is invalid!

Such an objection would be devastating to our argument, save for one bit of enlightening information. It is virtually without disagreement among biblical scholars that Mary as well as Joseph was "of the house of David" (Luke 1:27; cf. Luke 2:4). This blood relation of Mary to her forefather King David is corroborated by other Scripture (see Luke 1:32, 69; Matthew 9:27; 15:22; 20:30, 31; Mark 10:47, 48).

That Mary, as the woman who physically mothered Christ, was of David's line is foreshadowed in the prophecies that the promised Messiah was to be the very offspring of David as well as successor to the Davidic throne (cf. 2 Samuel 7:12ff.; 1 Kings 8:25-26; Isaiah 7:2, 13-14; 9:7; Jeremiah 23:5; 33:15, 17, 22, 25-26; John 7:42; Mark 11:10). The Apostle Paul wrote that "Jesus Christ ...descended from David" (2 Timothy 2:8), and furthermore states that Jesus Christ "was descended from David according to the flesh" (Romans 1:3).

Indeed, according to His own testimony, Christ Jesus Himself is both "the root and the offspring of David" (Revelation 22:15).

Now inasmuch as the references to women of Hamitic descent impact upon the "house of David," Jesus' lineage is so affected by virtue of Mary His mother. This is true in both the cases of Tamar and Rahab, for they preceded David and his house. Further, it may not be unreasonable to assume that Mary's bloodline may also have been influenced through Solomon, the son of Bathsheba and David. The fact that Luke's Gospel carries a heightened emphasis on the very physical descent of Christ gives an added strength to this argument.

So here we have it, Tamar, Rahab, and Bathsheba – each of Hamitic descent, each a lineal ancestor of Christ Jesus according to reliable genealogical information of Matthew's and Luke's Gospels. Ontologically and genealogically speaking, then, Jesus is Black, for "Black" ancestral blood ran in His human veins.

Such truth concerning the racial/ethnic identity of Jesus is liberating to many of us, despite the fact that racial relationship to Christ may serve for Black people only as a cordial invitation to Christ. It continues to stand that each person, of whatever racial-ethnic origin, must personally come to the Lord for salvation, regardless of a kinship relationship to Christ Jesus. Faith in the atoning death of Christ is the way to redemption from sin and to wholistic liberation; not a claim on physical/kindred relationship to Christ.[192]

C.

Summary

In this brief treatment of a subject which has a great significance for Black people, we have sought to demonstrate the Blackness of the Old Covenant Community of God. **The Old Covenant-Messianic community was Black, the Messianic line was Black, and the Messiah Himself was Black. Each separate treatment provides enough crucial data to stand on its own. However, taken together, these three lines of thought form a strong and convincing argument establishing the ontological, ethnological, ancestral, physical, actual,[193] and (in many cases) dark and colorful(!) Blackness of the Hebrew-Israelite-Judahite-Jewish people.**

The information provided above is not exhaustive. There are other Scripture data which could also be used to support our argument. For example, we could have made mention of the Cushite Egyptian names of members of Moses' family giving us an insight into their ethnology.[194] Or we could have made note of Joseph's and Mary's flight with Jesus into Egypt escaping the wrath of Herod. How could a "white" Christ be hidden among a Black people?[195]

Of course, there is also the extra-Biblical evidence which affirms, among other things, the Blackness of Christ Jesus. For instance, the earliest portrayals of Christ Jesus in art show Him and His mother Mary as Black in actual skin color.[196] This is the perception of Christ which was passed from one generation to another generation: it was a psychological/pictorial image of a physically Black Christ and His mother. The portrayals of a "white" Jesus were not given a great emphasis until the 15th century A.D. – hundreds of years after Christ's incarnation into humanity and His sojourn in the world.

Let the reader beware! Most of the pictorial images people have of the Biblical Hebrew-Israelite-Judahite-Jewish community indicate that these persons were and looked white. Furthermore, most of the images people have of this Covenant community indicate that they looked like the contemporary eastern European Jews who, in this 20th century, now inhabit the land of Palestine. According to Biblical and archaeological information, such ethnological images are incorrect. The Covenant community of the Scriptures contained a marked element of Blackness and many of them looked Black.[197]

The Persian Empire

—— Limit of the Persian empire c.500 B.C.
—— Persian royal road
• Royal residences
--- Red Sea-Nile canal built by Darius I

SECTION X

Summary and Directions

A. A Review

B. A Challenge

A.

A Review

At this point a summary of the ground we have covered may be useful. In **Section I** we dealt with definitions and terminology used in understanding the Bible's Black presence. We addressed the "Bible" which is the basis of our study. Christ Jesus is its subject, and redemption is its thrust. When properly understood, it serves as an accurate and reliable historical, cultural, and geographical record of Black people in the ancient world. We also shared our approach toward using Bible reference works and extra-Biblical writings to supplement and enlighten our research, and the need to give special attention to the studies of Blacks as they impact the subject.

In this section we further stated the importance of using both African and "Black," an ancient ethnological self-identifying term of Black peoples. We rejected the racist notion of so-called "Caucasoid Hamites," of "white Black" people. This study would not have been well-grounded had we neglected a definition of what we mean by "Black." It is three pronged including actual skin color, so-called "Negroid" characteristics, and ancestral "Black blood." We proceeded to explain that there is an explicit, implicit and presumed Black presence in the Bible. Each has its own place and is capable of clear exposition. The final thought in this section had to do with the transformation of Black identity through the redemption in Christ Jesus the Lord. This is our motivation throughout.

With **Section II** we covered the process of identification. The researcher can identify Biblical Blacks especially through their names and adjectives used to describe them, by their family trees, extra-Biblical information (archaeological, historical, cultural, anthropological and the like), and through chronological correlation with world history. The reader was encouraged to proceed from identifying obvious Blacks to tackling the identity of those needing more verification. Both individual persons and nations are gathered in the scope of this study. A "nation" may on the one hand be a highly organized geopolitical entity, and on the other hand be an "extended family," or tribe. We closed this section by providing some basic data on several Biblical Blacks.

The focus of **Section III** sought to impress us with the importance of the study of the Black presence in the Bible for especially Black people. It is historically, Christianly, spiritually and redemptively important. Toward communicating this study to the masses, we provided several ways by which popular conceptions of Blackness might be related to identifying Biblical Blacks.

A most important part of this writing is **Section IV** where we discussed the Table of Nations *(Genesis 10)* and the Hamitic Black/African genealogical line. In this section we were given an introduction and background to *Genesis 10*. This unique ancient document provides a look at the identity of ancient humanity, descended from Noah, through numerous and diverse names. Understanding the structure of this genealogical Table is crucial for fully appreciating its names and "notes," and the inter-relationships of ancient peoples. Among other things, the Table is both biological and multidimensional. Pertaining to descendants of Ham, the Table is a veritable "Black/African family tree," which sets the foundation for illuminating the Black presence in the Bible and reveals the prominent place in antiquity held by Black peoples.

Close on the heels of the previous section, **Section V** was given to Ham and Hamitic descendants. Here we discussed the Biblical significance of "Ham" and its relation to Egypt and other places in the Biblical world, and what we mean by "Hamitic." Our usage is Biblical/genealogical, not linguistic. Ham's sons/descendants were Cush, Mizraim (Egypt), Put, and Canaan – explicit Black nations. Each of these peoples and their descendants were Biblically and briefly exposited. The exposition was done in the context of the Table's names and structure.

The Cushite Black presence was found in Africa, Arabia and Asia. The Cushite Nimrod was exceptional. Mizraim's (Egypt's) presence was found in northern Africa (both Upper and Lower Egypt), Libya, Canaan, and the Mediterranean (Crete). The

Philistines were the offshoot of the Egyptian tribe Casluhim. The Putites were present either in Libya or east African Somaliland. The Canaanite Biblical Black presence was found in the land prior the Israelite conquest. Their tribes were numerous. Prime Canaanite peoples included both the Phoenicians and the Hittites of Canaan.

It was appropriate to close this section by wrestling with the issue of Ham's Blackness relative to his brothers, Shem and Japheth. The evidence at hand – including genetics, history, and archaeology – all point to a humanity originally Black with one component deriving into whiteness. All prototypical civilizations the world over were indigenously Black.

Cush was given special treatment in **Section VI**. We discussed African-Cush, south of Egypt, and Cush all over the Biblical world including Africa and Asia. "Cush" itself was an ancient identifying term of Black people, wherever they were found. The geography of Cush (Biblical Ethiopia) was compared/contrasted with modern Ethiopia. Biblical Ethiopia (Cush) was much wider than the modern connotation. We provided the basis for analyzing the inconsistent translation of "Cush" and "Ethiopia," and challenged the reader to think "Cush" when reading the *King James Version* mis-identifications.

Realizing that Black peoples are discoverable in other than the Hamitic genealogical line, and that all humanity is related by virtue of relationship to our common ancestor Noah, we provided a brief discussion of Non-Hamitic people in **Section VII.**

With **Section VIII** we returned to our major thrust and provided an overview of the Black world surrounding Biblical history, an Old Testament time-line of several Black persons, and a listing of several explicit New Testament Black persons.

Many think that the Black presence in the Bible is something outside the Biblical Covenant Community. This notion should have been dispelled through **Section IX** which dealt with the Blackness of the Old Covenant Community. We dealt with the Blackness of the

Hebrew-Israelite-Judahite-Jewish people. Both the Covenant-Messianic Community and the Messianic line itself possessed explicit Blackness. This set the tone for discussing the Blackness of the Messiah (Christ Jesus) Himself. His Blackness was demonstrable through His ancestors mentioned in His genealogy. His Blackness was ethnological, ancestral, physical and most likely dark and colorful.

B.

A Challenge

This study on the Black presence in the Bible is not exhaustive. As one may have ascertained, there are hundreds of explicitly Black persons in the Bible, and many more who may be presumed Black by virtue of the evidence presented. Our purpose has been to provide an overview of the subject so that those who are Christian Black educators – whether ministers, Church School teachers, directors of Christian education departments, Deans of Congresses and Conferences, seminary and Bible school professors, instructors of religion and ancient literature in institutions of higher learning, and all others engaged in education – will have a foundation on which to build. We have sought to lay a foundation that is Christ honoring, Biblically trustworthy, academically sound, and intellectually and emotionally digestible.

We would now encourage others to use this foundation to further their own research and teaching. Two appendices deal with basic research where the reader is led step by step into an authentic discovery process.

The psychological time is ripe and the people are longing for this kind of information. If prior to the year 2000 the message of the Bible's Black presence does not reach the majority of American Blacks, it will, in my opinion, be dishonoring to God and an exposure of the dereliction of Biblical Black educators. In addition we will have forfeited our privilege to exercise an option in the process of redemption that may mean the salvation of Black people, America, and even the world. Christ struggled, suffered and died to redeem humanity. Will we let Him down?

The Black presence in the Bible is multifaceted. It is Biblical, theological, historical, literary, cultural, archaeological, psychological, ethnological and spiritual. The Black presence in the Bible is also **eternal.** Jesus said, "Heaven and earth will pass away, but my words will not pass away" (Matthew 24:35). There is something of the eternal in what God has said about Black peoples in His Word. His Word is an "eternal gospel," to be proclaimed "to those who dwell on earth, to every nation and tribe and tongue and people" (Revelation 14:6). Since the Black presence in the Bible is eternal, though it concerns us, it is above us and beyond us. It transcends us and yet reaches us like no other word. The Lord's eternal Word can sustain us and is able to bear us from this transient existence of life into the eternal glorious dwelling places of God Himself. For His glory, to His praise. **There is an eternal Black presence in God.**

Appendices

Basic Research

Appendix I

How to Begin the Discovery Process

We know that there are Black people in the Bible, but how can we find out who they are? How can we identify them so that we can speak about them with confidence?

FIRST, start with what you know. The name "Africa" is not used in the Bible. But there are other names for Black people which are used there. Several of those names are "Ham," "Ethiopia," and "Egypt." This is the starting point. Let's work with "Ethiopia."

When you look up the name "Ethiopia" in an **English dictionary**, there you will find it has two basic meanings. One is a modern meaning, and the other is an ancient meaning. Since the Bible was written thousands of years ago, and records historical events much older, our concern would be with the ancient definition of the word "Ethiopia." Yet, just consulting an English dictionary will not tell us for sure which definition (the modern or the ancient meaning) we should use. Therefore, with your English dictionary, always be sure that in all of your Bible study you use a good **Bible dictionary.**

SECOND, with a **Bible dictionary** look up the word "Ethiopia." When you find the article you will notice that it shows the distinction between the ancient and the modern meaning of the word. Also, the article will provide a general discussion of the significance of the land and people of Ethiopia in Bible times. Various theological insights and related information will be given. As you read the article you will find that other people and lands are directly or indirectly related to "Ethiopia." For instance, your attention will be drawn toward "Cush," "Black," "Egypt," etc. This additional information will become branches of your study. What you will find most helpful in the article under study are additional Bible references. You should begin to keep a list of these verses.

THIRD, at this point you might want to make use of a **Bible atlas**. A Bible atlas (or a group of maps of Bible lands) is always useful. Within the atlas you will find two primary things. One, a time period map of the geographical area with which you are concerned. In this particular instance you will find a map of Africa and the Near East. And, two, general written information about the people who inhabited the targeted geographical area during the time period of your concern.

FOURTH, consult an exhaustive **Bible concordance**. You will use the concordance to look up verses with the word "Ethiopia," and other words you found related to your subject in the Bible Dictionary. As you look up the various words, you will find that your concordance (if it is a major concordance) gives different ways a particular word is used in various verses. You may choose to record all the references which you find, or only those which you think have a bearing on your subject of study.

Why are you looking up all these references? So that you can then look up and read all those verses in your Bible! Though this is a lot of work, it is nonetheless very rewarding. For as you continue this process, you are teaching yourself through firsthand research of the primary document – the Bible itself. Doing this gives you a great degree of enlightenment and personal confidence. Then you can speak with surety about your own discoveries. Also, you can verify the accuracy of what you have read in the Bible dictionary articles. If you have a Bible which has notes which are technical (in contrast to devotional) in nature, let them assist you. Those persons who do not research the Bible for themselves make themselves psychological captives to the judgments and opinions of others – whether good or bad.

FIFTH, use a **Bible handbook** to further your research. A Bible handbook will provide charts, study aids, and general contextual information which will help you to understand the verses you are studying. A Bible handbook serves as an informative and gentle guide. It doesn't tell you everything, but it tells you enough to keep you going in a good direction.

SIXTH, when you discover passages of Scripture which are hard for you to understand, then it is time to consult a **Bible commentary**. Good commentaries will provide you with detailed information and contrasting views on a given passage or point of controversy. Always seek to first understand the Scripture itself. Then allow the commentary to examine your findings. There are some things which you will take issue with in a commentary. At other times you will allow the commentator to correct you. At any rate, keep studying and learn all you can. When you get deep into your study you will find that you disagree with some things you thought at the beginning of your study.

SEVENTH, begin to consult specialized **Biblical reference works**, and other **books on the subject** – to obtain Biblical or extra-Biblical information. Head to the library, particularly a good library which contains a good collection of books written by Black authors. Or, if your budget can support it, head to the bookstore. If you are serious about your research you should find this area most challenging and fulfilling. Your discernment skills will be sharpened, your grasp of knowledge will be stretched, and your understanding will broaden. Keep notes on what you read. Most likely you will return to these works for more investigative adventures.

EIGHTH, **share** what you find. Preferably, use a paper you have written to teach a class on your chosen subject. In the future, this paper will become the groundwork for further study into the area. You may even write a book!

Following is a research guide and subject study format for studying the Black presence in the Bible. If you gain information for all categories under consideration, you will be blessed with a well-rounded knowledge of the particular subject under study.

Appendix II

Research Guide and Subject Study Format

Following is a study guide that may be used when studying about Black persons within the Scripture. If research is performed according to this format, the student will reap the fruit of gaining a broad understanding of any subject whose life is studied. With modifications, this guide may also be used in the study of Black nations within the Scripture.

I. Primary Biblical Reference

II. Name of Personage and Meaning

III. Evidence Supporting Subject's Blackness

IV. Argumentation

V. Commentary on the Subject in Scriptural Context

VI. Associated Scripture of a Theological Significance

VII. Extra-Biblical Information and Sources

VIII. Significance/Application for Black People Contemporarily

IX. Value to the Community of Faith and the Canon of Scripture

X. Questions and Leads for Further Study/ Issues that Demand Attention

XI. Manuscript preparation for Preaching and/or Teaching and/or Publication

Abbreviations

AV	Authorized Version (Same as King James Version)
BEB	Baker Encyclopedia of the Bible
EBD	Eerdman's Bible Dictionary
FAWNE	Funk and Wagnalls New Encyclopedia
IBD	Illustrated Bible Dictionary
ISBE	International Standard Bible Encyclopedia
KJV	King James Version
NASV	New American Standard Version
NBD	New Bible Dictionary
NIV	New International Version
NUBD	New Unger's Bible Dictionary
NUBH	New Unger's Bible Handbook
RSV	Revised Standard Version
ZPEB	Zondervan Pictorial Encyclopedia of the Bible

Notes

----

1. See the bibliography for some recently released titles. Our own work in the seminar manual has been around for several years and has undergone several revisions.

2. The purposes on which Dr. Copher and I agreed when conducting together our February 1990 seminar in Chicago were: 1) To glorify Christ Jesus our Lord; 2) To help Black people to specifically identify the Black and African persons in the Bible; 3) To assist Christians in applying to their lives practical lessons learned from Black Biblical models and teachings in the light of Romans 15:4 and 1 Corinthians 10:6, and 11; and 4) To effect within Black people a radical transformation of their Black identity from the spiritual ground of its roots in God, so that they will rise up for the cause of the liberation of themselves and for the redemption of the world by God through Christ Jesus the Lord. All to the glory of God.

3. During the "*Orientation*" session of one of our seminars, the participants were introduced to topics such as "**Ethnological Orientation**," "**Methodological Orientation**," "**Biblical Orientation**," and "**Geographical Orientation**." Following their orientation period, the participants were led into "*Foundations of the Bible's Black Presence*," which dealt with "**The Black World Surrounding Biblical History**," and "**Black People and the Origin of Humanity and Ancient Civilizations**."

4. Charles B. Copher. "Three Thousand Years of Biblical Interpretation with Reference to Black Peoples," *African American Religious Studies: An Interdisciplinary Anthology,* ed. Gayraud S. Wilmore, (Durham, North Carolina: Duke University Press, 1989), p. 105.

5. "Inasmuch as a curse of blackness whether upon Cain, or Ham, or Canaan does not appear in the biblical text, those who take the

Bible, including the Old Testament, to be the Word of God, norm for faith and practice, would appear to be engaging in **blasphemy** when they substitute interpretations." Copher. *Ibid.*, p. 124 (my emphasis).

6. "...you have been acquainted with the sacred writings which are able to instruct you for salvation through faith in Christ Jesus. All Scripture is inspired by God and profitable for teaching, for reproof, for correction, and for training in righteousness, that the man of God may be complete, equipped for every good work" (2 Timothy 3:15b-17). "First of all you must understand this, that no prophecy of scripture is a matter of one's own interpretation, because no prophecy ever came by the impulse of man, but men moved by the Holy Spirit spoke from God" (2 Peter 1:20-21).

7. Father Clarence Williams, "Search: The Black People's Presence in the Bible," (video transcript), *Search: The Black People's Presence in the Bible*, exec. prod. Father Clarence Williams, (Detroit, MI: Search, 1987), p. 7.

8. Recommended reading for a concise but intensive treatment of the role of "context" in Biblical exegesis and the formulation and articulation of theology is William H. Bentley, *The Significance of Context in Black Theology*, (Chicago: National Black Christian Students Conference, 1980).

9. For hundreds of years the Bible was the **primary** Book used for the study of ancient history.

10. Egyptian civilization, however, predates Sumerian civilization. See Runoko Rashidi, "More Light on Sumer, Elam and India", *African Presence in Early Asia*, (Journal of African Civilizations Ltd., Inc.), eds. Ivan Van Sertima and Runoko Rashidi, (New Brunswick, NJ: Transaction Books, 1985, 1988), p. 163; Rashidi remarks "...it seems rather obvious that the bright light of Sumerian civilization can only be attributed to the arrival of Black migrants from Africa's Nile Valley." The Sumerians "were only one of the numerous Nilotic Kushite colonies implanted in early Asia." "Africans in Early Asian

Civilizations: A Historical Overview," *African Presence in Early Asia*, (Journal of African Civilizations Ltd., Inc.), eds. Ivan Van Sertima and Runoko Rashidi, (New Brunswick, NJ: Transaction Books, 1985, 1988), p. 15; Finch remarks: "Nile Valley civilizations exercised a cultural hegemony over all of Western Asia in antiquity." "For many centuries, large parts of Western Asia were either under Egypt's direct political control or in a state of vassalage to her." "...the Sudanic civilizations of Cush and Ethiopia also left an imprint on their Western Asiatic neighbors." "If the Nile Valley civilizations of Egypt and Cush were the world's oldest, if language first became codified there, if written literature first appeared there, if Western Asian cultures were created by Nile Valley colonists to one degree or another..." Charles S. Finch III, M.D., "Africa and Palestine in Antiquity," *African Presence in Early Asia*, (Journal of African Civilizations Ltd., Inc.), eds. Ivan Van Sertima and Runoko Rashidi, (New Brunswick, NJ: Transaction Books, 1985, 1988), pp. 188-189; see also John G. Jackson, *Ethiopia and the Origin of Civilization*, pp. 17-18, for a presentation of the relationship between Sumer, Akkad and African Cush.

11. Refer to later section, "The Blackness of Original Humanity and Prototypical Civilizations."

12. Merril F. Unger "suggests that a very early home of the Hamitic Cushites was in the land of Shinar, the Biblical counterpart of cuneiform *Sumer(u)* or Sumer, where Nimrod raised them to prominence. From there the Cushites may well have extended their power by merchants or armies to the Yemenite region of Arabia, and then crossed the narrow Red Sea to invade the Sudan area and impose their name on that entire district." *Zondervan Pictorial Encyclopedia of the Bible*, 1st ed. (1975), s.v. "Nations," by J. Rea. Unger's position is that "the Cushites migrated to Africa (Kosh or Nubia)." Merill F. Unger, *The New Unger's Bible Handbook*, rev. Gary N. Larson, (Chicago, IL: Moody Press, 1984), p. 40.

13. Diop states "...of necessity the earliest men were ethnically homogeneous and negroid." "...there were only two routes available by which these early men could move out to people the other

continents, namely, the Sahara and the Nile valley." Cheikh Anta Diop, "Origin of the Ancient Egyptians," *General History of Africa: Ancient Civilizations of Africa*, ed. G. Mokhtar, 8 vols., (Berkeley, CA: University of California Press, UNESCO, 1981), vol. 2: p. 27.

14. Rashidi states "The blacks were also the first in the development of Asia's early civilizations." "Ancient Sumer, the Biblical land of Shinar, was the formative civilizing influence of early West Asia." "...it seems rather obvious that the bright light of Sumerian civilization can only be attributed to the arrival of Black migrants from Africa's Nile Valley." "In their own literature the Sumerians called themselves 'the black-heads,' and were only one of the numerous Nilotic Kushite colonies implanted in early Asia." Runoko Rashidi, "A Historical Overview," *Op. cit.*, pp. 14-15; Custance presents Sumer as one of the basic centers of civilization which he says underlie all others. "Each of these cultural centers of the early world was Hamitic in origin." He cites the self-identification of Sumer as "the blackheaded people"; literally, "the head-of-black people." He also cites Hammurabi's Code of Laws which too refers to the Sumerians as "the blackheaded ones." Arthur C. Custance, *Noah's Three Sons: Human History in Three Dimensions, vol. 1: The Doorway Papers*, (Grand Rapids, MI: The Zondervan Corporation, 1975.), pp. 98, 151.; Diop asserts, "It can be concluded from the foregoing, that from 5 million years ago to the glacial thaw 10,000 years ago, Africa almost unilaterally peopled and influenced the rest of the world." Cheikh Anta Diop. "Africa: Cradle of Humanity," *Nile Valley Civilizations*, ed. Ivan Van Sertima, (New Brunswick, NJ: Journal of African Civlizations Ltd., 1985), p. 27.; "From the anthropological point of view...the human race first came into existence in Africa in the region of the sources of the Nile." Cheih Anta Diop, "Annex to Chapter I: Report of the symposium on 'The Peopling of Ancient Egypt and the Deciphering of the Meroitic Script'," *Op. cit.*, p. 61.

15. Chancellor Williams comments that "The periodization of African history is carefully arranged in such a way that the history becomes the history of Arabs and Europeans in Africa, and not the history of Africans...*There is no period of Black civilization* in Black

Africa. Such is the Caucasian viewpoint – almost a religion." Chancellor Williams, *The Destruction of Black Civilization: Great Issues of a Race from 4500 B.C. to 2000 A.D.,* (Chicago, Illinois: Third World Press, 1976.), p. 39.; Note the title of Diop's work: *The Cultural Unity of* **Black** *Africa,* (Chicago, Illinois: Third World Press, 1978) (my emphasis); "It is thus clear that it was the whole of the Egyptian population which was negro, barring an infiltration of white nomads in the protodynastic epoch." "There are about nine centuries between the birth of Aeschylus and Herodotus and the death of Ammianus Marcellinus, nine centuries during which the Egyptians, amid a sea of white races, steadily crossbred. It can be said without exaggeration that in Egypt one household in ten included a white Asiatic or Indo-European slave." Cheikh Anta Diop, "Origin of the Ancient Egyptians," *Op. cit.*, pp. 30, 39.

16. The reader should consult the following words and article by a W.S. LaSor for a good(!) racist example of this point. The position of its author is ambiguous, inconsistent, and fraught with the fear of the truth regarding Black people. Following is a representative quote from the author: "There is no evidence, either in the Bible or in extrabiblical material, to support the view that Ham or any of his descendants was negroid. The Greek term *Aithiops* does indeed mean 'burnt face,' and was doubtless applied to peoples to the south of Egypt because of their dark complexion. However, both the Ethiopians and the Nubians lack the physical characteristics, other than skin pigmentation, that are used anthropologically to define the negroid peoples. Of the identifiable descendants of Ham named in Genesis 10 all are caucasoid. The first reference to the Negroes is found in late Egyptian records." *The International Standard Bible Encyclopedia.* (rev. 1979-1988), s.v. "Cush," by W. S. LaSor.

17. Charles B. Copher, "The Black Man in the Biblical World," *The Journal of the Interdenominational Theological Center,* vol. 1, no. 2 (Spring 1974): 7.

18. Charles B. Copher, "Blacks and Jews in Historical Interaction: The Biblical/African Experience," *The Journal of The Interdenominational Theological Center,* vol. 3, no. 1 (Fall 1975): 10.

19. "The Egyptians had only one term to designate themselves: ...*kmt* = the negroes (literally)." "*KMT* was the strongest term existing in the language of the pharaoh's to indicate blackness..." "This word gave rise to the term 'Hamite' which has been much used subsequently. It is also found in the Bible in the form 'Ham'." Diop, "Origin of the Ancient Egyptians," *Op. cit.*, pp. 41, 62. Note the pointed contrasting response to Diop's position by one of his respondents: "...*KM*... meant 'black'..." "The form *KMTYW* could mean only two things: 'those of Kmt', 'the inhabitants of Kmt' ('the black country'). It was a derived adjective (*nisba*) formed from a geographical term which had become a proper name; it was not necessarily 'felt' with its original meaning..." "To designate 'black people', the Egyptians would have said *Kmt* or *Kmu,* not *Kmtyw.* In any case, they never used this adjective to indicate the black people of the African hinterland whom they knew about from the time of the New Kingdom onwards; nor, in general, did they use names of colours to distinguish different peoples." S. Sauneron, "Report of the Symposium," *Op. cit.*, p. 64. Though the previous views clash as to the intensity and use of *KMT*, there is no question that the Egyptian term under discussion obviously references a strong dimension of "blackness." In the Biblical tradition, "Ham" which we believe means "Black," is naturally associated with Egypt. Notice Psalm 78:51, "He smote all the first-born in Egypt, the first issue of their strength in the tents of Ham." Psalm 105:23, "Then Israel came to Egypt; Jacob sojourned in the land of Ham." In a differing vein on the ancient usage and signficance "Black" as an ethnological identification descriptive of actual identity, Custance, citing Gadd in his *Sumerian Reader,* says that "the idea of 'men' as real people by contrast with other human beings who are not really men at all" was the implied meaning and usage of "blackheaded people" (used by the Sumerians of themselves) who were proud of their black skin. Custance, *Op cit.*, p. 152.

20. Many anthropologists have traditionally divided humanity into three "races:" Caucasoid, Negroid, and Mongoloid; each of these three broad divisions having its own subgroups. These classifications are all modern, occuring within the last three hundred years or so. The self-identification of Blacks by their skin color is a

practice which is thousands of years old.   J.A. Rogers wrote "Scientists...claim to see in the color of the human skin something so important as to warrant establishing mankind into separate and distinct races – white race, red race, black race, brown race, brunette race, blond race, etc., etc., etc. For nearly three hundred years they have been dinning 'Race, Race, Race,' into the ears of humanity. The books they have written on the subject would tower miles into the sky. One does not exaggerate." J. A. Rogers, *Sex and Race: Negro-Caucasian Mixing in all Ages and All Lands. Vol. 1 - The Old World.* (St. Petersburg, FL: Helga M. Rogers, 1967), pp. 6-7; "Most history texts, especially the ones on ancient history, start off by telling us that there are either three, four or five races of man, but that of those races only one has been responsible for civilization, culture, progress and all other good things.   The one race is of course the white race, and particularly that branch of said race known as the Nordic or Aryan." John G. Jackson, *Ethiopian and the Origin of Civilization,* (Baltimore, MD: Black Classic Press, 1939), p. 4; Jackson goes on to identify persons who number the races of humanity as 5: 1) European (white), 2) African (black), 3) Asiatic (yellow), 4) American (red) and 5) Oceanic (brown), and one person who conceived of 29 differing racial groups; see: Diop, *Great African Thinkers: Vol 1. Cheikh Anta Diop,* eds. Ivan Van Sertima, Larry Williams. (New Brunswick, NJ: Transaction Books, 1986), p. 235ff.; *ZPEB*, s.v. "Race," by M. K. Mayers.

21. "After the rise and decline of Greek civilization and the Roman destruction of the City of Carthage, they made the conquered territories into a province which they called, 'Africa,' a word derived from 'afri,' and the name of a group of people about whom little is known. At first the word applied only to the Roman colonies in North Africa."   John Henrik Clarke,   "Social Studies African-American Baseline Essay," *African American Baseline Essays,* (consul. ed.) Dr. Asa G. Hilliard (Portland, OR: Portland Public Schools, 1989), pp. ss 1-2.; The continent which was called "Africa" by the Greeks and Romans formerly was called "Ethiopia, Corphye, Ortegia, Libya, Olympia, Hefperia, Oceania, and Ammonis." **"Alkebu-lan'** is the oldest, and the only [name] of indigenous origin. It was used by the Moors, Nubians, Numidians,

Khart-haddans [Carthagenians], and Ethiopians. 'Africa,' [is] the current misnomer adopted by almost everyone today..." Yosef A.A. ben-jochannan, *Black Man of the Nile: and His Family,* (Baltimore, MD: Black Classic Press, 1989), p. 47.; see ben-jochannan, *Africa, Mother of Western Civilization,* (Baltimore, MD: Black Classic Press, 1988), p. 679.

22. "Black," used as a popular racial/ethnic color-term, refers to "dark skin pigmentation," characteristic of predominantly African, Oceanian, and Australian peoples and their descendants. See *The Random House Dictionary of the English Language,* 2nd ed. unabr. (1987) s.v. "Black."

23. Copher, "Search: The Black People's Presence in the Bible," *Op. cit.,* p. 3.

24. According to William H. Bentley, the most basic commonality, the cohesive, which ties together the Black group is color, whether "Black, Brown,...Beige...or all the in-between shades." He sees color as a racial and ethnic classification, and "a feature of unqualified commonality in the establishment of Black identity" with its ethnic common denominator being our "undeniable element of 'Africanity'." He goes on to say that this Black Africanity is for many a "creative positive, rather than a burden to be borne." William H. Bentley, *Defining and Identifying the Black Group,* (Chicago: National Black Christian Students Conference, 1980) pp. 2-3.

25. Our attention may be drawn to a photo by James Brunson appearing in the *African Presence in Early Asia.* It shows Jewish prisoners taken captive in Palestine by the Assyrians around 700 B.C. These prisoners are definitely negroid. Likewise, there is a photo appearing in the *Illustrated Bible Dictionary* of a Sumerian, the people who inhabited the land of "Shinar" mentioned in Genesis 10:10; 11:1; 14:1, 9; Isaiah 11:11; Daniel 1:2; Zechariah 5:11. It depicts Gudea, Governor of Sumer (@ 2150 B.C.). His negroid features are prominent. "Ethnologically, upon the basis of criteria established by white men, the color black may have nothing to do

with race. A Negro is one who exhibits a certain group of traits which include black color, a particular type of hair, and skeletal structure, especially cranial." Copher, "The Black Man in the Biblical World," *Op. cit.*, p. 9. It should be understood that the anthropological criteria for determining "Negroidness" is not absolute. If the criteria for who is Negroid is applied to an all white population, a certain percentage of these peoples will turn out to be "Negroid!" The criteria is somewhat "elastic." See Diop, "Africa: Cradle of Humanity," *Op. cit.*, pp. 28-29.

26. Copher, "The Black Man in The Biblical World," *Op. cit.*, p. 9.

27. See Genesis 41:50-52; 1 Chronicles 7:14-19; 7:20-29; Numbers 26:28-37.

28. See 1 Chronicles 3:1-24; Matthew 1:6ff.; Luke 3:23-31ff.; *ZPEB*, s. v. "David."

29. "In the United States whites known to have any amount of 'Negro blood' – no matter how small – are classified as Negroes; in Africa, North Africa in particular, they do the very opposite. Blacks with any amount of 'Caucasian blood' are classified as 'White.' This scheme was rigorously applied in the history of Egypt, for example, where even unmixed black pharaohs became 'white' and the originally black population was never referred to as Egyptians at all!" Williams, *Op. cit.*, p. 39. In America the precise definition of Black "may vary from state to state; or the definition may be one set by the Federal Government. Nationally, anyone with a discernible trace of African Negro blood is a black." Copher, "The Black Man in the Biblical World," *Op. cit.*, p. 9.

30. "Negro...is often used pejoratively, however, as a means of expressing social prejudice. In such circumstances the person referred to need have relatively little Negroid ancestry." *Funk & Wagnalls New Encylopedia*, (1975), s.v. "Negro," by W.C.G.

31. The Mormons and others have spoken of "one drop" (!) of Black blood as the qualifying distinctive of blackness.

32. A Biblical hermeneutic, a principle used as a rule for Biblical understanding and explanation.

33. See Diop, "Origin of the Ancient Egyptians," *Op. cit.*, p. 39.

34. "...the patriarch Abraham migrated from what later came to be called Chaldea, a land occupied by Cushites." Copher, "Blacks and Jews in Historical Interaction: The Biblical/African Experience," *Op. cit.*, p. 12. See: Rashidi, "A Historical Overview," *Op. cit.*, pp. 17-19; Rashidi, "More Light on Sumer, Elam and India," *Op. cit.*, pp. 168-169.

35. See Bishop Alfred G. Dunston, Jr., *The Black Man in The Old Testament and Its World*, (Philadelphia, PA: Dorrance & Company, 1974), chapt. vi., "The Mixed Multitude," pp. 58ff.; R. Alan Cole, *Exodus: An Introduction and Commentary, Tyndale Old Testament Commentaries*, gen. ed. D. J. Wiseman, (Downers Grove, IL: Inter-Varsity Press, 1973), p. 87. See his comment on Exodus 6:16: "There may well have been much intermarriage in early days (Genesis 41:45)."

36. Concerning Crete, it is usually assumed that the Cherethites of David's bodyguard were Cretans (2 Samuel 8:15-18; 15:18; 1 Chronicles 18:14-17), and the name Caphtor (from whence came the Philistines) is a reference to Crete (Deuteronomy 2:23; Jeremiah 47:4; Amos 9:7; Genesis 10:14). Were these elite fighters Black? Consider the following by Snowden: "Egyptian tomb paintings have preserved other vivid representations of Nubians who served at various times under Egyptians...From the south also had come Ethiopians (Kushites) who had overrun Egypt and ruled it for more than half a century. It was perhaps via Egypt that the blacks, depicted on a Minoan fresco, had come to Crete to serve as auxiliaries" Frank M. Snowden, *Blacks in Antiquity*, (Belknap Press: Cambridge, MA, 1970), p. 119.; see Drusilla Dunjee Houston, *Wonderful Ethiopians of the Ancient Cushite Empire*, (Baltimore, MD: Black Classic Press, 1985); notice Houston's citation from *The Earth and Its Inhabitants, vol. 1, p. 306* associating ruins in Cush with those in Crete: "...whose tunnel shaped gallaries like those of Crete

are still to be seen passing under the houses."; Copher states, "...Blacks, including Negroes, during Biblical times, inhabited...parts of Arabia, Phoenicia, Canaan, Crete and Greece" Copher, "Blacks and Jews in Historical Interaction: The Biblical/African Experience," *Op. cit.*, p. 11.; also "...David employed Philistine mercenaries who had come from Crete where Black troops had been in service since early Minoan times, having come from Ethiopa and Egypt" Copher, "Egypt and Ethiopia in the Old Testament," *Nile Valley Civilizations,* ed. Ivan Van Sertima (New Brunswick, NJ: Journal of African Civlizations Ltd., 1985), p. 173 and notes; Hansberry states, "...evidence was found which seemed to indicate that at various intervals in the long history of Minoan civilization there were evidently direct contacts with people and cultures of black or African origin. Evidence of such intercommunications dates from the very beginnings of the early Minoan civilization..." William Leo Hansberry, *Africa & Africans as Seen By Classical Writers,* ed. Joseph E. Harris (Washington, D.C.: Howard University Press, 1981), sec. "The Aegean and Africa," p. 35.; R.K. Harrison, *Introduction to the Old Testament,* (Grand Rapids, MI: William B. Eerdmans Publishing Company, 1969), p. 312.

37. Two of the Biblical inhabitants of Cyprus were Barnabas (Acts 4:36), and Bar-Jesus (Acts 13:6ff.). Could it be verified that either of the forementioned were Black?! Contact of Blacks with the island of Cyprus occurred at various historical points. It was conquered by Thutmose III of the 18th Dynasty (1501-1447 B.C.); it was influenced much by Crete; the Phoenicians made settlements on the island in the 9th and 8th c. B.C.; it was conquered by Aahmes (Amasis) of Egypt and held to 526 B.C.; it fell under the domain of the Ptolemies of Egypt (323 B.C.); and again under their domain in 294-258 B.C. See *ISBE,* s.v. "Cyprus," by M. N. Tod and R. A. Gwinn; *Baker Encyclopedia of the Bible,* (1988), s.v. "Cyprus."; Clarke, "Social Studies African-American Baseline Essay," *Op. cit.,* sec. "The Ptolemaic Period - 332-47 B.C.," p. SS-43; Snowden has written: "The most convincing explanation of Negroid stone figures found in Cyprus is that the sculptures were portraits of Ethiopians in the civil and military service of the Egyptains during Egyptian occupation of the island under Amasis [king of Egypt] (568-525

B.C.)." "A striking piece of corroborative evidence for the presence of Ethiopians in Cyprus is the traditional opinion of the Cyprians themselves, recorded by Herodotus, that one component of their population was Ethiopian. The combined literary and archaeological evidence, together with the fact that Egyptians had a long history of recruiting Ethiopians, tends to confirm the view that the figures depicted Negroes present during the military occupation of Cyprus in the sixth century. It is not possible to determine the size of the Negroid contingents among the Egyptian forces, but it does not seem likely that the Cyprians would have included Ethiopians in a statement of population statistics – the others mentioned being Salaminians, Athenians, Arcadians, Cythnians, and Phoenicians – had the numbers been negligible." Snowden, *Blacks in Antiquity,* (Cambridge, MA: Belknap Press, 1970), pp. 121, 122-123; see also notes and pp. 24-25, 101, 157 and fig. 1, p. 33.

38. See James E. Brunson, *Black Jade: African Presence in the Ancient East,* intro. by Runoko Rashidi (DeKalb, IL: KARA Publishing Co., 1985), part iv., "The African Presence in the Ancient Mediterranean and Aegean Isles", pp. 123-135.

39. In the Biblical geographical world, Blacks were to be found in Arabia, Elam-Persia, Mesopotamia, Greece, India, Phoenicia, Crete, Cyprus, and Canaan, Egypt and Cush.

40. Commenting on Exodus 6:14-27 dealing with Moses' and Aaron's genealogical line, we read: "*Merari* may be an Egyptian name. Such names are very frequent in the tribe of Levi, whatever the explanation: Moses and Putiel ...are other examples" Cole, *Op. cit.,* p. 87.; "Moses was of black Cushite origin. Support for the opinion comes in the form of Egyptian names carried by members of the family as well as by other Hebrews: Moses, Phinehas, Hophni, Merari, Pashur, etc., especially Phinehas, which means Black, Negro, Nubian, etc." Copher, "Blacks and Jews in Historical Interaction: The Biblical/African Experience." *Op. cit.,* p. 13.

41. For example, see Judges 3:1-6. "...in prehistoric times, before the coming of the Hebrews to Canaan, and also during the time of

Hebrew-Israelite-Jewish occupation, Negroid peoples lived in the land, apart from any black element in the Hebrew-Israelite-Jewish population." Copher, "Blacks and Jews in Historical Interaction: The Biblical/African Experience," *Op. cit.*, p. 11.; "...from 8,000 B.C. – the era of the Natufian Blacks of Canaan – to 3500 B.C., most of Western Asia, including Canaan, Mesopotamia, and the Arabian Peninsula, was inhabited more or less exclusively by a black people. In Canaan, these were the above-mentioned Natufians," Finch, *Op. cit.*, p. 188.; Custance says Sennacherib, the king of Assyria (r. 705-681 B.C.) refers to the Canaanites as "blackness of head people" in his famous six-sided prism. This is the term which the indigenous population of Sumer (Biblical "Shinar") used with reference to themselves. Custance, *Op. cit.*, p. 152; see p. 72 and notes.

42. For instance Tamar the Canaanite (Genesis 38:26ff.; Matthew 1:3); Rahab the Canaanite (Joshua 2:1; 6:25; Matthew 1:5); Bathsheba the wife of Uriah the Hittite (2 Samuel 11:3; Matthew 1:6) and Athalia, daughter of Ahab and Jezebel the Sidonian, the granddaughter of Omri (the sixth king of the northern kingdom of Israel), who married Jehoram king of Judah, and became the mother of Ahaziah (Jehoahaz), king of Judah (1 Kings 16:29-31; 2 Kings 8:25-27; 11:1-3; 2 Chronicles 22:1-9).

43. A rather expansive category of evidence for identifying Blacks in the Biblical world is presented by Copher. Namely, archeaological data; modern historical works; critical Biblical scholarly works; personal names and adjectives; opinions of modern travelers, archaeologists and anthropologists; ancient Greek-Roman legends and historical writings; works of early Christian commentators; and ancient Jewish writings. See Copher, "Blacks and Jews in Historical Interaction: The Biblical/African Experience." *Op. cit.*, p. 11.

44. See Diop, "Origin of the ancient Egyptians," *Op. cit.*, sec. "Witness of the Bible," p. 43.

45. When referencing Blacks in the Bible we can refer to "Cushite Blacks," "Egyptian Blacks," "Putite Blacks," and "Canaanite Blacks." Each of these descendants of Ham, except perhaps the Putites, had

extensive dealings and contacts with the Covenant community in the Old Testament and are mentioned numerous times throughout the Scripture. Why should these peoples and their descendants not receive proper racial/ethnic identification, and their Biblical data not be exegeted?

46. See sec. "Special Cushite Discussion" appearing later.

47. "All scripture is inspired by God and profitable for teaching, for reproof, for correction, and for training in righteousness, that the man of God may be complete, equipped for every good work" (2 Timothy 3:16-17).

48. See Copher, "Blacks and Jews in Historical Interaction: The Biblical/African Experience," *Op. cit.*, p. 11.

49. "Names provide a means of indicating specific identity, and as such are essential to efficient communication about times and circumstances involving individual people and places. Proper names are therefore found most frequently in the historical portions of the Old Testament..." "The naming of persons in Old Testament times obviously went beyond a concern for a convenient means of providing individual designation. Naming intended to capture in some way the essence of an individual, expressing actual identity rather than merely identification." *ISBE,* s.v. "Names, Proper," by D. Stuart.

50. Genesis 25:13; Psalm 120:5; Song of Solomon 1:5. It means "exceedingly Black," according to Copher, "Search: The Black People's Presence in the Bible," *Op. cit.*, p. 4.; See also Copher, "Three Thousand Years," *Op. cit.*, p. 107; *Eerdmans Bible Dictionary,* (1987) s.v. "Kedar." Perhaps a secondary meaning of "Kedar" is "mighty." So it could be said that the Kedarites were **"Black and mighty!"** See *NUBD,* s.v. "Kedar."

51. Exodus 6:25; 1 Chronicles 9:20; see Copher, "Three Thousand Years," *Op. cit.*, p. 107.; *Illustrated Bible Dictionary,* (1980) s.v. "Phinehas," by K.A. Kitchen.

52. "Ethiopia" 2 Chronicles 16:8; 21:16; Isaiah 20:4; see Copher, "Three Thousand Years," *Op. cit.*, p. 107.

53. Jeremiah 2:16; 43:7, 8, 9; 44:1; 46:14; see. *IBD,* s.v. "Tahpanhes"; Copher, "Blacks and Jews in Historical Interaction: The Biblical/African Experience," *Op. cit.,* p. 15. See also Cushan and Ham as place names.

54. Genesis 14:5; 1 Chronicles 4:40; see Copher. "Three Thousand Years," *Op. cit.,* p. 108; *EBD,* p. 456; s.v. "Ham"; *ISBE,* s.v. "Ham."

55. Acts 13:1; *A Greek-English Lexicon of the New Testament and Other Early Christian Literature,* William F. Arndt and F. Wilbur Gingrich. (Chicago, Illinois: University of Chicago Press, 1957.), p. 541; s.v. "Niger"; *ISBE,* s.v. "Niger"; note *The Living Bible* rendering, "the Black Man."

56. See Snowden, who cites what appears to be the correct translation of the verse, which none of the popular modern versions (KJV, RSV, NASB, or NIV) captures. *Blacks in Antiquity,,* pp. 198-199, 331. Following are the other translations of Song of Solomon 1:5: "I am black, but comely, O ye daughters of Jerusalem, as the tents of Kedar, as the curtains of Solomon" (KJV). "Dark am I, yet lovely, O daughters of Jersalem, dark like the tents of Kedar, like the tent curtains of Solomon" (NIV). "I am very dark, but comely, O daughters of Jerusalem, like the tents of Kedar, like the curtains of Solomon" (RSV). "I am black but lovely, O daughters of Jerusalem, Like the tents of Kedar, Like the curtains of Solomon" (NASV).

57. Copher, "Egypt and Ethiopia in the Old Testament." *Op. cit.,* p. 173.

58. See articles on "Elam." *ZPEB,* by A.C. Schultz; "Elam, Elamites." *ISBE,* by A.R. Millard.

59. Rashidi informs us that "...Elamite cultural forms, their goddesses, art-motifs, weapons and scripts, link them back to the

Nile Valley so that one could actually speak of Elam as 'a Kushite colonoy with its Susiana heartland'." Van Sertima, "Editorial," *Op. cit.*, p. 8.; see also pp. 19-22.; see Rashidi, "More Light on Sumer, Elam and India," *Op. cit.*, pp. 170-171.; Runoko Rashidi, "The Nile Valley Presence in Asian Antiquity," *Nile Valley Civilizations,* ed. Ivan Van Sertima, (New Brunswick, NJ: Journal of African Civlizations Ltd., 1985), pp. 209-213.; Houston, "Ancient Media and Persia were Cushite," *Op. cit.*, p. 255ff.

60. "...the descendants of Shem cannot be expected all to have spoken one language, or even to have lived in one area, or even to have belonged to one racial type, since intermarriage may have obscured this." Mitchell, *Op. cit.*; Windsor opines: "All the children of Shem were black." Rudolf R. Windsor, *From Babylon to Timbuktu: A History of the Ancient Black Races Including the Black Hebrews,* (Smithtown, NY: Exposition Press, 1969), p. 19.; "As for the sons of Ham being black because of a curse, we shall see later that in all probability the sons of Shem, from whom the Jews are supposed to be descended, were black themselves. *According to the Bible, the eldest son of Shem was Elam, and the Elamites as we have just seen were a black people*" Rogers, *Sex and Race*, p. 60., p. 19., see pp. 58-60.

61. See Copher, "Blacks and Jews in Historical Interaction: The Biblical/African Experience," *Op. cit.*, p. 14 and notes; John T. Carson, "Zephaniah," *The New Bible Commentary: Revised,* eds. D. Guthrie, J.A. Motyer (Grand Rapids, MI: William B. Eerdmans Publishing Co., 1970), p. 775.

62. Refer to Rea, *Op. cit.*, p. 375ff. Factors in ancient perceptions of nationhood include: ethnicity, territory, theology, politics, and linguistics. The kinship emphasis of nationhood was expressed as (a) a kinship concept; (b) all male relatives; (c) all male members of the clan, tribe, or settlement; (d) all citizens or members of the community; (e) the entire nation, including women and children. That Black peoples of the Bible were regarded by their kinship bonds is evidenced from such Scriptures as "...Blessed be Egypt my people, and Assyria the work of my hands, and Israel my heritage"

(Isaiah 19:25). The political emphasis of nationhood is applied to a variety of entities: pre-Israelite Canaanite tribes (Deuteronomy 7:1), bedouin-type desert tribes (Isaiah 60:5ff.), city-states (2 Kings 19:13), nation-states (e.g. Israel), and larger imperial states (Egypt, Babylon, Jeremiah 25:17ff.).; Block, *Op. cit.*, pp. 492-496.

63. This information is based on the *Revised Standard Version*.

64. "Cush" and "Ethiopia" refer to one and the same people. See the "Special Cushite Discussion."

65. Gathering and examining such Biblical data is essential for those who would do first-hand research of the subject at hand. In many instances these names can be traced from one passage of Scripture to another and studied in a thematic manner. Though the mention of individual names varies in frequency, some of them are found numerous times in the Bible. Using an exhaustive concordance we are able to trace each of these names through the Bible, locating each verse and passage in which they are used. For a good example of this type of analysis, one might refer to Copher's article "Egypt and Ethiopia in the Old Testament," *Op. cit.*, pp. 163ff.

66. This information is provided only for a cursory examination. Its careful study is suggested. For instance, whereas the untranslated name "Asshur" is mentioned only 5 times, "Assyria," is mentioned 131 times. Also, "Sheba" and "Dedan" are names associated with not only Cush, but also with Jokshan, a descendant of Abraham and Keturah (Genesis 25:3; 1 Chronicles 1:32).

67. Some of the references have double occurrences of a name. Also, these persons may be alluded to in other passages of Scripture without their names being given.

68. "He is the source of your life in Christ Jesus, whom God made our wisdom, our righteousness and sanctification and redemption" (1 Corinthians 1:30). "In him we have redemption through his blood, the forgiveness of our trespasses, according to the riches of his grace which he lavished upon us" (Ephesians 1:7). See also

Romans 3:24; Hebrews 9:12.

69. Matthew 27:33-36; Mark 15:23-26; Luke 23:33-34; John 19:17-18.

70. "For our sake (God) made him to be sin who knew no sin, so that in him we might become the righteousness of God" (2 Corinthians 5:21).

71. Notice the emphasis on kindred relationships, ethnicity, and national identification in the following verses from *Revelation.* "...and they sang a new song, saying, 'Worthy art thou to take the scroll and to open its seals, for thou was slain and by thy blood didst ransom men for God from every tribe and tongue and people and nation and hast made them a kingdom and priests to our God and thy shall reign on earth'" (Revelation 5:9-10). "After this I looked, and behold, a great multitude which no man could number, from every nation, from all tribes and peoples and tongues, standing before the throne and before the Lamb, clothed in white robes, with palm branches in their hands, and crying out with a loud voice, 'Salvation belongs to our God who sits upon the throne, and to the Lamb!'" (Revelation 7:9, 10). "Then I saw another angel flying in midheaven, with an eternal gospel to proclaim to those who dwell on earth, to every nation and tribe and tongue and people; and he said with a loud voice, 'Fear God and give him glory, for the hour of his judgment has come; and worship him who made heaven and earth, the sea and the fountains of water'" (Revelation 14:6-7).

72. "Additionally, one may be defined as black regardless of color or race; all who suffer oppression, especially oppression at the hands of white Westerners, are classified as black" Copher, "The Black Man in the Biblical World," *Op. cit.,* p. 8. Copher cites Arthur Weigall, a scholar who calls Tirharkah and other Egyptian Pharaohs "nigger kings." Copher, *Ibid.,* p. 16.

73. See Snowden, *Op. cit.,* pp. 198-199, 331.

74. When Moses fled Egypt he went to the desert of Midian. The Midianites were a Black people. When Joseph and Mary fled with

Jesus from the wrath of Herod, they went into Egypt, Africa. See Exodus 2:15; Habakkuk 3:7; Matthew 2:13ff. See Dunston, *Op. cit.*, p. 97ff.; Houston, *Op. cit.*, pp. 127, 167.; *ISBE*, referring to an archaeological discovery connecting Midian to Egypt, s.v. "Midian, Midianites," by T.V. Brisco.

75. *ZPEB*, s.v. "Genesis," by H. C. Leupold.; *ISBE*, s.v. "Table of Nations," by D. I. Block, p. 708; *NUBD*, p. 464. For a differing outline see also R. K. Harrison, *Introduction to the Old Testament*, (Grand Rapids: Eerdman's Publishing Company, 1969), p. 548ff.

76. For example, the Chinese are not mentioned in the Table, nor the aboriginals of Australia. Neither are the Blacks who were in America B.C. That is, Before Christ as well as Before Columbus! Refer to Mitchell. *Op. cit.*, p. 1058. Van Sertima dates the time of Blacks in America from 948-680 before the Christian era. Ivan Van Sertima, *African Presence in Early America*, (Journal of African Civilizations Ltd., Inc.,) (New Brunswick, NJ: Transaction Books, Rutgers – The State University, 1987), p. 15. See also sec. "Egypto-Nubian Presences in Ancient Mexico." pp. 29-55. In contrast, others would discover the Chinese under the Hamitic line. See Custance, *Op. cit.*, p. 105ff.

77. See Block, *Op. cit.*, p. 712; J. Rea, *ZPEB*, sec. "A. The Table of Nations. 1. Introduction" p. 376.

78. Refer to the complementary volume for a complete discussion.

79. This word is used often in Genesis and in other places throughout the Old Testament. One can compare its use in Genesis 5:1 and Matthew 1:1, two passages in which the phrases used bear a close resemblance. See *IBD*, s.v. "Generation," by T. C. Martin.

80. The phrase "These are the sons of Japheth" is added by *RSV* for balance. See 10:20 and 31. The *KJV* and the *NIV* omit the phrase which is lacking in the Hebrew.

81. See Ross, *Op. cit.*, sec. "Variation of Style," p. 225f.; Westermann, *Op. cit.*, p. 502; Block, *Op. cit.*, sec. "B. Genealogical Formulas," p. 708.

82. "Son of" could indicate "son of," "grandson of," and "descendant of." "Became the father of" could mean to "bear" in the physical sense, but also, "became the ancestor of." See Martin, *Op. cit.*, p. 546, 547. "The terms for 'son' and 'become the father of' in these formulas may legitimately be interpreted more loosely as 'descendant' and 'become the ancestor of'." Block, *Op. cit.*, p. 708.
Even when these terms are used to establish actual physical relationship, the relationship may not in fact be immediate. For example, the "wording that by Amram Jochebed 'bore' Moses, Aaron and Miriam (Exodus 6:20; Numbers 26:59), like 'became the father', *AV* 'begat', in Genesis 5 and 11, need not imply immediate parenthood but also simply descent. Compare Genesis 46:18, where the preceding verses show that the great-grandsons of Zilpah are included among 'these she bore to Jacob'." Kitchen *Op. cit.*, p. 270. "A remarkable Egyptian example is a brief text in which King Tirhakah (c. 670 B.C.) honours his 'father' Sesotris III (c. 1870 B.C.) who lived some 1200 years before him." See Martin, *Op. cit.*, p. 547, who also provides additional examples.
The marginal reading for the *NIV* dealing with "son of" in Genesis 10:2, 3, 4, 6, 7, 20-23, 29 and 31 reads "*Sons* may mean *descendants* or *successors* or *nations*." It goes on to read in reference to "became the father of," found in Genesis 10:8, 13, 15, 24 and 26, "*Father* may mean *ancestor* or *predecessor* or *founder*." Wenham, *Op. cit.*, p. 215; Ross, *Op. cit.*, p. 224.

83. Also, see 1 Chronicles 2:51 where, in a genealogical passage, Salma (an individual person) is called the "father of Bethlehem" (a city). Ahaz told Tiglath-Pilser, according to 2 Kings 16:7, "I am your servant and your son."

84. Understanding the Biblical concepts of "nation" is integral to pinpointing this latter emphasis. The reader is referred to *ISBE*, s.v. "Nations," by Block. See in particular "I. O.T.–Terminology."

85. "Mizraim" in *KJV*; used four times: Genesis 10:6, 13; 1 Chronicles 1:8, 11. This normal Hebrew term is one of the plural gentilics found in the Table. Untranslated, it conforms to the other names in the list of descendants of "Egypt," the translated term.

86. The use of "kingdom" (10:10) is obviously political. A kingdom is not necessarily homogeneous and often contains a multiplicity of ethnic entities.

87. Though the use of "race/racial" terminology in respect to the Table seems inappropriate and therefore should be avoided, the significance of the hereditary and biological connections indicated by such terminology is evident and essential for establishing the Black/African "family tree."

88. "A racial classification is given to a group of individuals who share a certain number of anthropological traits, which is necessary so that they not be confused with others. There are two aspects which must be distinguished, the phenotypical and the genotypical." Cheikh Anta Diop, *Great African Thinkers,* ed. Ivan Van Sertima, (New Brunswick, N.J.: Transaction Books, 1986), p. 235. According to genotype, "A race is a human population that is sufficiently inbred to reveal a distinctive genetic composition manifest in a distinctive combination of physical traits." "The Bible does not refer to the term "race"; nor is there a concept of race developed in the Bible." *ZPEB,* s.v. "Race," by M. K. Mayers. According to Diop, the phenotype, which involves a definite combination of distinguishing physical traits, is "what really counts."

89. "If this table simply assigns fabled ancestors to the various nations, then there are exegetical problems with the tradition of Genesis. The chapter includes famous people, well-known cities and places, tribes and nations, as well as a number of names that could be individuals but are known later as peoples. Since the word 'eponymous' is used so widely for the mystical personages of pagan traditions, it seems inappropriate for Genesis, for these biblical traditions not only rejected mythical concepts but frequently included polemics against them. But if the word can be limited to its

basic meaning of a founder or ancestor who gave his name to the people or place, then there is no problem, for that view does not call the tradition into question." Ross, *Op. cit.,* p. 223f.

90. Mitchell, *Op. cit.*, p. 1056.

91. See Martin, *Table of Nations*, p. 815.

92. "It is important to note that [these]...names could have different meanings at different points in history, so that the morphological identification of a name in Genesis 10 with one in the extra-biblical sources can be completely valid only if the two occurrences are exactly contemporary." "...There are three principal characteristics of a people which are sufficiently distinctive to form some nuance of their name. These are race or physical type; language, which is one constituent of culture; and the geographical area in which they live or the political unit in which they are organized." Mitchell, *Op. cit.,* p. 1056.; see also Rasmussen, *NIV Atlas,* sec. "Toponyms: Study of Place Names," p. 204f., for insights and variables involved in attaching ancient names to specific places on a modern map.

93. Review the section: "'Black': An Ancient Ethnological Self-Definition."

94. Rasmussen, *Op. cit.,* p. 237. As an archaelogical discovery, Ham is a city about "10 miles east of Beth-shean on the King's Highway between Ashterorthkarnaim and Shaveh-kiriathaim." This place may or may not be the exact location of the "Ham" of Genesis 14:5. *ISBE,* s.v. "Ham," by G. A. L.

95. It would also be clear if the Scripture meant that the descendants of "Ham (in Canaan)" were "Mizraim," "the two red mud lands." However, this translation would run contrary to the understanding that humanity's and civilizations roots are traceable back to Egypt's Nile Valley. Also, notice "the **tents** of Ham" in Psalm 78:51. It appears to be intensive and stresses habitat (originally in tents?). In contrast, "the **land** of Ham" is more extensive of Egypt as a whole.

96. Refer below to section "Mizraim (The Egyptians)" for further insights.

97. Semitic languages include Akkadian, Arabic, Aramaic, Ethiopic, Hebrew, and Phoenician. "It is necessary to observe that names have been adopted from this chapter [Genesis 10] for certain specific uses in modern times. Thus in language study the terms 'Semitic' and 'Hamitic' are applied....This is a usage of convenience, however, and does not mean that all the descendants of Shem spoke Semitic languages or all those of Ham Hamitic." Mitchell, *Op. cit.*, p. 1056.

98. Ethiopic is a subdivision of Semitic languages that includes Amharic, Tigre, Tigrinya, and Geez. *Random House Dictionary*, s.v. "Ethiopic."

99. *ISBE*, s.v. "Canaan; Canaanites," sec. "VI. Language," by C.G. Libolt. The sources used to study the Canaanite language are Ugaritic texts, the Amarna Tablets, and names from Egyptian sources.

100. The "term *Hamitic* has come to be applied by anthropologists and ethnologists in a rather restricted way to a group of people which it seems evident from Genesis 10 by no means now represents all the nations that can with justification be traced back to Ham. So I have to remind the reader that I am reverting, in my use of the terms Hamite and Hamitic, to their older and strictly biblical meaning." Custance, *Op, cit.*, p. 11.; "Hamitic" is defined as 1. "(especially formerly) the non-Semitic branches of the Afroasiatic language family." 2. "of or pertaining to the Hamites or Hamitic." *Random House Dictionary*.

101. *IBD*, s.v. "Ham," by T.C. Mitchell. Keep in mind that the author is referencing the genotype definition of race, not the phenotype.

102. "In general, the peoples to the South of the Near East are indicated in this list." Mitchell, *IBD*, p. 1057.; Wenham, *Op. cit.*, p. 214.

103. Wenham, *Op. cit.,* p. 221; *IBD,* s.v. "Put, Phut" by K. A. Kitchen.

104. See Ozzie Edwards, "Are Black People Cursed by God?" *Direction: Student,* 11, 12 (Chicago, IL: Urban Ministries, Inc.), 1981.

105. "The sheer length of this section indicates its importance. Among the sons of Ham are some of Israel's closest neighbors, who exercised a profound influence on her political and cultural life. This section sets these relationships in context." Wenham, *Op. cit.,* p. 219.

106. "There was then a woman, queen of Egypt and Ethiopia; she was inquisitive into philosophy, and one that on other accounts also was to be admired. When this queen heard of the virtue and prudence of Solomon, she had a great mind to see him..." "So when this queen of Ethiopia had obtained what we have already given an account of, and had again communicated to the king what she brought with her, she returned to her own kingdom." Flavius Josephus, *The Works of Flavius Josephus: The Wars of the Jews; The Life of Flavius Josephus; Antiquities of the Jews.* trans. William Whiston, A.M., 4 vols. (Grand Rapids, MI: Baker Book House, 1974, 1986.) sec. VIII.VI.5, "How Solomon...entertained the Queen of Egypt and of Ethiopia." pp. 510-514; *ISBE,* s.v. "Sabeans," by W. S. LaSor.

107. See Westermann, *Op. cit.,* p. 511 for sources.

108. Refer to the complementary volume for a detailed discussion of Nimrod.

109. Translated "all of them" in the *RSV.*

110. Wenham, *Op. cit.,* p. 223.

111. Josephus, *Op. cit., Antiquities* I.VI.4.; Wenham, *Op. cit.,* p. 230. He goes on to say that neither were the Elamites a Semitic people.

112. Refer to complementary volume for documentation.

113. See James Brunson, "The African Presence in the Ancient Mediterranean Isles and Mainland Greece," in *African Presence in Early Europe*. pp. 36-65.

114. Frank M. Snowden, *Blacks in Antiquity*, (Belknap Press: Cambridge, MA, 1970), p. 119. Note also the following comments in connection with the Black foundations of both Crete and Cyprus. Be wary of the author's misleading labeling of "Shem," "Ham," "Japheth," etc. "Herodotus (vii:90) relates that [Cyprus] was first colonized by Phoenicians (Shem), Ethiopians (Ham), and Greeks (Japheth). This would be similar to the situation on the island of Crete where a Semitic people who had come by way of Egypt (Minoans) were eventually displaced by Indo-Europeans from Greece (Myceneans). Probably a similar situation prevailed on Cyprus, although being nearer the Phoenician homeland, the Greek influence took longer to become dominant." *ZPEB*, s.v. "Kittim," by J. Oswalt.

115. Josephus, *Antiquities*. sec. I.VI.2. *Op. cit.*.

116. For a discussion of the issue see *ISBE*, s.v. "Put," by W. S. LaSor; *ZPEB*, s.v. "Put," by F. B. Huey, Jr.

117. *ZPEB*, s.v. "Canaan, Canaanites," by J. Arthur Thompson.

118. The "merchant," "trader" use of Canaan may have very ancient roots. See *ZPEB*, s.v. "Canaan," by C. G. Libolt. The term "Canaanite" is traceable in Job 41:6; Isaiah 23:8; Ezekiel 17:4; Hosea 12:7; Zephaniah 1:11; Zechariah 11:7, 11.

119. Libolt, *Op. cit.*, p. 585.

120. Libolt, *Op. cit.*, p. 587.

121. Rea, *Op. cit.*, "Nations," p. 282.

122. If so, the name means "'client of Ges [the Sumerian god of light],' ...[whose] worship was introduced into Phoenicia and Palestine ca. 2000 B.C." Wieand, *Op. cit.,* p. 472.

123. The questionable evidence has to do with the "assumption" that textual scribes made mistakes in spelling "Hivite" instead of "Horite" or "Hurrian," and that no people named the "Hivites" is found in extra-Biblical sources, an argument from silence. (In passing, it is interesting that concurrently a dissociation is made between the "Hivites" and the "Hittites." See *EBD,* s.v. "Hivites."; *ZPEB,* s.v. "Horite," by H. A. Hoffner, Jr.) Refer to *ISBE,* s.v. "Horites," by F. W. Bush for a critical discussion. See complementary volume for a fuller discussion of the issues.

124. See Morris, *Op. cit.,* p. 255f.; Custance, *Op. cit.,* pp. 105-107.

125. *NUBD,* s.v. "Zemarites."

126. Libolt, *Op. cit.,* p. 586.

127. Note the references to "families" (clans or tribes) and "nations" within the verses of Genesis 10:1, 5, 20, 31, 32. Genesis 10 is neither primarily racial nor individual, but ethnological.

128. "...Elamite cultural forms, their goddesses, art-motifs, weapons and scripts, link them back to the Nile Valley so that one could actually speak of Elam as 'a Kushite colony with its Susiana heartland'." Van Sertima, "Editorial," *Op. cit.,* p. 8; see also pp. 19-22.; Rashidi, "More Light on Sumer, Elam and India," *Op. cit.,* pp. 170-171.; Rashidi, "The Nile Valley Presence in Asian Antiquity," *Op. cit.,* pp. 209-213.; Houston, *Op. cit.,* sec. "Ancient Media and Persia were Cushite" p. 255ff.

129. The author believes in the Biblical doctrine of creation over against certain theories of evolution.

130. John Tierney, Linda Wright, Karen Springen, "The Search for Adam & Eve: Scientists Explore a Controversial Theory About

Man's Origins," *Newsweek,* 11 January 1988, pp. 46-52.

131. "We now know how the white man was formed, he was the most recent." Diop, *Great African Thinkers,,* p. 235. Compare 120,000 years ago for Black origination to 10,000 years ago for white development, according to Diop.

132. "And he [God] made from one [Adam] every nation of men to live on all the face of the earth, having determined allotted periods and the boundaries of their habitation, that they should seek God, in the hope that they might feel after him and find him. Yet he is not far from each one of us," (Acts 17:26-27).

133. Diop, "Origin of the Ancient Egyptians,"*Op. cit.,* p. 27.

134. Particularly so if one accepts the view of the global Flood which would have made marked changes in the geography of the world.

135. But notice the association of "Cush" with "Havilah," each locatable on the African mainland.

136. However, in reference to the river Gihon and Genesis 2:13 we read, "The referent of *kus* in Genesis is a vexing problem, however. In Genesis 2:13 it is rendered 'Ethiopia' (cf. also the AV) by the LXX [Septuagint], which apparently understood Gihon to be another name for the Nile (cf. Jeremiah 2:18, LXX; also Josephus *Ant.* i.1.3). To this day Ethiopians refer to the Nile springs as 'Giyon,' the Ethiopic word for Gihon." *ISBE,* s.v. "Ethiopia," by R. F. Youngblood. A well written and insightful article.

137. See Jackson, *Ethiopia and the Origin of Civilization,* p. 6.

138. Diop, *Great African Thinkers*, p. 130ff. Notice Diop's comparison and conclusion in the sec. "Could Egyptian Civilization be of Asian Origin?"

139. Diop, *Ibid.,* p. 235.

140. Rashidi quoting Diop, "More Light on Sumer, Elam and India," *Op. cit.*, p. 163.

141. Custance, *Op. cit.*, p. 98.

142. "The vestiges of this early [Cushite] civilization have been found in Nubia, the Egyptian Sudan, West Africa, Egypt, Mashonaland, India, Persia, Mesopotamia, Arabia, South America, Central America, Mexico, and the United States." "It was southern colored peoples everywhere, in China, in Central America, in India, Mesopotamia, Syria, Egypt and Crete who gave the northern white peoples civilization." Jackson, *Op. cit.,* p. 9, and p. 10, quoting a Bishop William Montgomery Brown.

143. Zephaniah 3:10; Psalm 87:4; Ezekiel 29:10; Esther 1:1.

144. *ZPEB,* s.v. "Ethiopia," by J. Alexander Thompson. Herodotus was the Greek historian of the 5th Century, B.C.; so-called the "Father of History."

145. Hansberry, *Africa & Africans,* p. 9.

146. The Nile begins in Central Africa (the white Nile) and in the Ethiopian highlands (the Blue Nile) and flows north through Egypt; It is mentioned 31 times in the Old Testament, especially in connection with Israelites in Egypt and in prophetic oracles. See Carl G. Rasmussen, *Zondervan NIV Atlas of the Bible,* (Grand Rapids, MI: Regency Reference Library. Zondervan Publishing House, 1989), secs. "The Geography of Egypt," pp. 57ff., "Nile," p. 247.; John Rogerson, *Atlas of the Bible,* (New York, NY: Facts on File Publications, 1985,), sec. "Egypt," p. 217; Van Sertima, *Egypt Revisited,* (New Brunswick, NJ: Journal of African Civilizations Ltd., Inc. Transaction Publishers, 1989), p. 425.; *IBD.* s.v. "Nile," by K. A. Kitchen; *FAWNE,* s.v. "Nile."

147. Dunston, *Op. cit.,* p. 22.

148. Houston, *Op. cit.,* sec. "Synopsis of Contents," p. i.

149. Houston, *Ibid.*, p. 40ff.

150. See Job 28:19 where the book mentions the "topaz of Ethiopia." The experience of Job may be dated somewhere around the time of Abraham. It was at this time that the topaz of Ethiopia was already well-known. "It seems likely that Job himself lived in the second millennium B.C. (2000-1000) and shared a tradition not far removed from the patriarchs. Job's longevity of 140 years and his position as a man whose wealth was measured in cattle possessions, and the picture of roving Sabean and Chaldean tribesmen fits the 2nd millenium better than the first." *ZPEB*, s.v. "Job," by S. Barabas.

151. Houston, *Op. cit.*, pp. 44-45.

152. Houston, *Op. cit.*, p. 51.

153. Dunston, *Op. cit.*, p. 98.

154. Hansberry, *Africa & Africans.*

155. Hansberry, *Ibid.*, pp. 6-7.

156. Paul W. Coats in Houston, *Op. cit.*, p. ii.

157. Asa G. Hilliard in Houston, *Op. cit.*, p. 1.

158. See Houston, *Op. cit.*, "Introductory Note," "Synposis of Contents," and "Afterword."

159. Jackson, *Op. cit.*, p. 8. On the basis of Herodotus and other sources Jackson further affirms that "the Western Ethiopians who dwelled in India, were black in complexion, but that the Africans had curly hair, while the Indians were straight-haired...The aboriginal black inhabitants of India are generally referred to as the Dravidians...[and] the Ethiopians were considered as occupying all the south coasts of both Asia and Africa." p. 8.

160. Copher, "The Black Man in The Biblical World," *Op. cit.*, p. 9.

161. The *Talmud* is the collection of Jewish law and tradition consisting of the Mishnah and the Gemara and being either the edition produced in Palestine A.D. around 400 or the larger, more important one produced in Babylonia A.D. around 500. The *Midrashim* are early (espcially the first ten centuries A.D.) Jewish interpretations of or commentaries on a Biblcal text, clarifying or expounding a point of law or developing or illustrating a moral principle.

162. Copher, "Blacks and Jews in Historical Interaction: The Biblical/African Experience," *Op. cit.*, p. 11.

163. William Leo Hansberry, *Pilliars in Ethiopian History*. ed. Joseph E. Harris (Washington, D.C.: Howard University Press, 1974, 1981), p. 27.

164. Hansberry, *Africa & Africans,* pp. 9, 11.

165. There were other terms which the Ethiopians used to differentiate various geographical areas of their country. Hansberry goes on to mention "*Kenset*" - Nubia; "*land of Alu*" - the general region to the south as far as the juncture of the Blue and the White Niles; "*land of Athi (ye)*" - an important division of the northern country; and "*land of Yesbe*" - regions to the south. *Africa & Africans.*, p. 9.

166. Dunston, *Op. cit.*, pp. 18-24.

167. Dunston, *Op, cit.*, pp. 15-16, 21.

168. Refer to previous section.

169. "If translations of the text are to be useful for the purpose of Biblical studies, they must, besides being faithful to the [text], be contemporary and even indigenous to a particular people. It is this point, more than any other, which manifests the truth that translations are a base for the [explanations] of exegesis. For in seeking to be contemporary and even indigenous, translations not

only tell what the text says, but also tell, in part *what the text means*! In other words, there is some interpretation involved in every translation. Whether it is implicit or even explicit, *it is there*. The nature of 'translation' makes this practice unavoidable, and even insures that its presence is felt." Walter Arthur McCray, *Who Says God Says?! A Black Perspective Examining the Authority of New Testament Exegesis by Highlighting the Foundation for Its Interpretations and Applications*, (Chicago, IL: Black Light Fellowship, 1980), p. 12.   "...all translation is by its very nature also interpretation." Copher, "Three Thousand Years," *Op. cit.*, p. 106.

170. "Cush." *ZPEB,* s.v. "Cush," by H. C. Leupold, refer to sec. "1. Confusion corrected."; Dunston, *Op. cit.,* p. 21f.

171. Dunston, *Ibid.,* pp. 18, 20.

172. In passing, this point is pertinent to the use of "Black" as a racial-ethnic identification of African originated people mentioned in the Scripture.

173. Dunston, *Op. cit.,* p. 18.

174. See Wenham, *Op. Cit.,* pp. 228, 201. Ham, however, should not be classified as the youngest son of Noah, which some scholars erroneously do based on Genesis 9:24 and 10:21.

175. *IBD,* s.v. "Table of Nations."

176. The people of Lud(im) referenced in Genesis 10:6 with Egypt, are regarded by some to be Hamitic.

177. The Aramaeans may be a reference to Blackness in Shem's line. They were a west Semitic-speaking semi-nomadic people who were known from cuneiform sources to have been constantly infiltrating into Syria and Mesopotamia from almost the whole of the Arabian desert-fringe. The terms "Syria/Syrian" should not be used of these people prior to 1000 B.C. *IBD,* s.v. "Aram, Aramaeans," by K. A. Kitchen. See connections between Aram, Elam and Assyria in

Genesis 10:22-23 and Amos 9:7. In Isaiah 22:6 Qir is used for Assyria along with Elam. Compare also Cushan-Rishathaim king of Aram-naharaim (Mesopotamia) with Judges 10:6.

178. Mitchell, *Op. cit.,* p. 1058.

179. Copher, "The Black Man in the Biblical World," *Op. cit.,* p. 9.

180. Cushan-Rishathaim from Mesopotamia falls within the Judges period.

181. Some scholars date the Judges period longer. There are differing chronological systems when dating Old Testament events. According to the "early Exodus and long Sojourn" in Egypt, the Conquest of Canaan and the Judges period would be 1406-1050 B.C. For the "early Exodus and short Sojourn," the period would also be 1406-1050 B.C. A "late Exodus" would make the Conquest of Canaan and the Judges period fall within 1230-1025. The same would hold true for the "Reconstructionist" chronological system which dates the Patriarchal age very late. See John H. Walton, *Chronological and Background Charts of the Old Testament,*" (Grand Rapids: Zondervan Publishing House, 1978), sec. "Comparison of Chronological Systems," and "Date of the Exodus," pp. 25, 29-30. For extensive discussions on the dating of Old Testament events refer to the following articles written from contrasting perspectives: *ZPEB,* s.v. "Chronology of the Old Testament," by J. B. Payne; *IBD,* s.v. "Chronology (OT)," by K. A. Kitchen and T. C. Martin.

182. Refer to sec. above, "The Definition of Blackness Used in the Study."

183. Copher, "The Black Man and the Biblical World," *Op. cit.,* p. 8.

184. *IBD,* s.v. "Chaldea, Chaldeans," by D. J. Wiseman.

185. Copher, "Blacks and Jews in Historical Interaction: The Biblical/African Experience," *Op. cit.,* p. 12.; see Genesis 10:8-10.; "The art, science and culture of the earlier unmixed Chaldeans was

Cushite." "It was universally attested by antiquity that from the Cushite element sprang the civilization of Chaldea." Houston, *Op cit.*, pp. 163, 164., and Chap. XI "The Strange Races of Chaldea," p. 160ff.; Rashidi, "A Historical Overview," *Op. cit.*, p. 15ff.

186. Van Sertima, "Editorial," *Op. cit.*, p. 8.; see Rashidi, "A Historical Overview," *Op. cit.*, p. 17.; Diop, "Origin of the Ancient Egyptians," *Op. cit.*, p. 29.

187. "The evidence at hand demonstrates beyond all reasonable doubt that they who were called 'the children of Israel' were a heterogeneous people, with no single bloodline, and predominantly of non-Hebrew or non-Asian descent." Dunston, *Op. cit.*, p. 69. and pp. 94ff.

188. *IBD*, s.v. "Marriage," by J.S. Wright and J.A. Thompson.

189. Her sister is called a Canaanitess in 1 Chronicles 2:3, 4.

190. The Hittites of Canaan are to be distinguished from the Indo-European Hittites who bore the same name. The Hittites, descendants of Heth, are referred to as "the people of the land" (Genesis 23:7) dwelling in Hebron in Abraham's time (see Genesis 23:2ff). *IBD*, s.v. "Hittites," by F.F.Bruce.; *ZPEB*, s.v. "Canaan, Canaanites." by J. Arthur Thompson.

191. The Greek term describing Mary's sexual state is very explicit: <u>parthenos</u>, Matthew 1:23; Luke 1:27. Mary had no husband, and had never had sexual relations. Such is the witness of the Scripture (Luke 1:34-35; Matthew 1:18ff.).

192. Romans 9:1ff.; 10:1ff.

193. In contrast to symbolical, conceptual, or metaphorical.

194. Copher, "Blacks and Jews in Historical Interaction: The Biblical/African Experience," *Op. cit.*, p. 13.

195. Matthew 2:13-23.

196. William Mosley, *What Color Was Jesus?*, (Chicago, IL: African American Images, 1987), pp. 12ff., 19ff.; Rogers, *Op. cit.*, Appendix to Chapters I to IX – Part II "The Black Madonna and The Black Christ.", pp. 273-283.

197. The Judahite-Jewish community of faith became increasingly whitenized under the domination of the Greeks and the Romans, particularly during the inter-testamental period and beyond.

Selected Bibliographical Sources

Listed below are several sources which bear upon either volume of **The Black Presence in the Bible: The Teacher's Guide,** or **The Table of Nations.** Some of these works either completely or in part directly address the subject. Others contain related reference material. Included the reader will find the works of Blacks and whites, recent and not-so-recent writers, Christians and non-Christians, Biblical scholars and lay persons, "liberals," "conservatives," "fundamentalists," and "evangelicals." Pertaining to the specific subject, this bibliography is not comprehensive. It does however reflect both the wide interest in the *Black presence in the Bible* and the wide-ranging impact it has on other disciplines.

Adamo, David Tuesday. *Black Women in the Bible.* By the Author, 1987.

_____. *The Black and The Israelite in the Period of King Hezekiah.* By the Author, 1987.

_____. *The Black Princes Who Delivered Prophet Jeremiah in the Bible.* By the Author, 1987.

_____. *The Black Prophet in the Bible.* By the Author, 1987.

_____. *The Black Secretary in the Bible.* By the Author, 1987.

Archer, Gleason L., Jr. *A Survey of Old Testament Introduction.* Rev. ed. Chicago: Moody Press, 1974.

Arndt, William F., Gingrich, F. Wilbur. *A Greek-English Lexicon of the New Testament and Other Early Christian Literature.* Chicago: University of Chicago Press, 1957.

Baker's Bible Atlas, ed. by Charles F. Pfeiffer. Grand Rapids: Baker Book House, 1973.

Baker Encyclopedia of the Bible, ed. by Walter A. Elwell. Grand Rapids: Baker Book House, 1988. See specific articles.

Baldwin, Joyce G. *The Message of Genesis 12-50.* Downers Grove, IL: Inter-Varsity Press, 1986.

Barrett, Leonard. *The Rastafarians.* Boston: Beacon Press, 1977.

ben-jochannan, Yosef A. A. *Africa: Mother of Western Civilization.* Baltimore: Black Classic Press, 1988.

_____. *Black Man of the Nile and His Family.* Baltimore: Black Classic Press, 1989.

Bennett, Jr. Lerone. *Before the Mayflower.* Chicago: Johnson Publishing Company, 1976.

Bentley, William H. *Defining and Identifying the Black Group.* Chicago: National Black Christian Students Conference, 1980.

_____. *The Significance of Context in Black Theology.* Chicago: National Black Christian Students Conference, 1980.

Bible Visual Resource Book. Ventura, CA: Gospel Literature Publications, Regal Books, 1989.

Bright, John. *A History of Israel.* 3rd ed. Philadelphia: Westminster Press, 1981.

Bruce, F.F. *Israel and the Nations.* Grand Rapids: Eerdmans, 1969.

Brunson, James E. *Black Jade: African Presence in the Ancient East.* DeKalb, IL: Kara Publishing Co., 1985.

_____. "An Interview with John G. Jackson." In *African Presence in Early Asia.* Rev. ed. New Brunswick: Transaction Books, 1988.

_____. "The African Presence in the Ancient Mediterranean Isles and Mainland Greece." In *African Presence in Early Europe*, ed. by Ivan Van Sertima. New Brunswick: Transaction Publishers, 1988.

Carruthers, Jacob H. *Essays in Ancient Egyptian Studies.* Los Angeles: University of Sankore Press, 1984.

Carter, LeRoy H. *Black Heroes of the Bible.* Chester Township, PA: Bethesda Press, 1982.

Champollion, Jacques. *The World of the Egyptians.* Minerva, S.A., Geneve, 1971.

Clarke, John Henrik. "Social Studies." In *African-American Baseline Essay.* Consultant Asa G. Hilliard. Portland: Portland Public Schools, 1989.

Collins, Paul. Hartman, Hermene D. *Great Beautiful Black Women: Portraits and Word Portraits.* Chicago: Johnson Products Company, 1978.

Copher, Charles B. "Blacks and Jews in Historical Interaction: The Biblical/African Experience". *The Journal of the Interdenominational Theological Center* vol. 3, no. 1 (Fall, 1975): 9-16. Also in *African Presence in Early Asia.* Rev. ed. New Brunswick: Transaction Books, 1988.

_____. "The Black Man in the Biblical World." *The Journal of the Interdenominational Theological Center* vol. 1, no. 2 (Spring 1974): 7-16.

_____. "Three Thousand Years of Biblical Interpretation with Reference to Black Peoples." *The Journal of the Interdenominational Theological Center* vol. 13, no. 2 (Spring 1986): 225-246.; In *African American Religious Studies*, ed. by Gayraud S. Wilmore. Durham and London: Duke University Press, 1989.

_____. "Egypt and Ethiopia in the Old Testament." In *Nile Valley Civilizations*, ed. Ivan Van Sertima. New Brunswick: Journal of African Civilizations, 1985.

Custance, Arthur C. *Noah's Three Sons: Human History in Three Dimensions.* Grand Rapids: Zondervan Publishing House, 1975.

Davis, John J. *Moses and the Gods of Egypt.* Grand Rapids: Baker Book House, 1971.

Diop, Cheikh Anta. "Origin of the ancient Egyptians." In *General History of Africa*, vol 2. "Report on the symposium on 'The Peopling of Ancient Egypt and the Deciphering of the Meroitic Script'," ed. G. Mokhtar. Berkeley: United Nations Educational, Scientific and Cultural Organization, 1981.

_____. *The African Origin of Civilization, Myth or Reality.* New York: Lawrence Hill & Company, 1974.

_____. *The Cultural Unity of Black Africa.* Chicago: Third World Press, 1978.

_____. *Great African Thinkers*, by Ivan Van Sertima. New Brunswick: Transaction Books, 1986.

_____. "Africa: Cradle of Humanity." In *Nile Valley Civilizations*, ed. Ivan Van Sertima. New Brunswick: Journal of African Civilizations, 1985.

Drake, St. Clair. *Black Folk Here and There.* Los Angeles: Center for Afro-American Studies, University of California, 1987.

Dunston, Bishop Alfred G., Jr. *The Black Man in the Old Testament and Its World.* Philadelphia: Dorrance & Company, 1974.

Eerdmans Bible Dictionary. (1987) Grand Rapids: Wm. B. Eerdman's Publishing Company. See specific articles.

Edwards, Jefferson D. *Chosen, Not Cursed.* 2nd ed. Kansas City, MO: Vincom, 1989.

Edwards, Ozzie. "Are Black People Cursed by God?" In *Direction, Student.* Chicago: Urban Ministries, Inc., 1980-1981.

Evangelical Commentary on the Bible, ed. Walter A. Elwell. Grand Rapids: Baker Book House, 1989.

Felder, Cain Hope. *Troubling Biblical Waters: Race, Class, and Family.* Maryknoll, NY: Orbis Books, 1989.

Finch, Charles S. III. "Africa and Palestine in Antiquity." In *African Presence in Early Asia.*" Rev. ed. New Brunswick: Transaction Books, 1988.

Finegan, Jack. *Myth and Mystery: An Introduction to the Pagan Religions of the Biblical World.* Grand Rapids: Baker Book House, 1989.

_____. *Light from the Ancient Past: The Archaeological Background of Judaism and Christianity.* 2 vols. London: Oxford University Press, 1959.

Gowan, Donald E. *Genesis 1-11: From Eden to Babel.* Grand Rapids: Eerdmans Publishing Company, 1988.

Green, Richard L., Ragsdale, Phyllis W., Lewis, Mary C. eds. *A Salute to Historic African Kings and Queens.* Chicago: Empak Enterprises, Inc. 1988.

Hansberry, William Leo. *Africa & Africans as Seen By Classical Writers*, ed. by Joseph E. Harris. Washington, D.C.: Howard University Press, 1981.

_____. *Pillars in Ethiopian History*, ed. by Joseph E. Harris. Washington, D.C.: Howard University Press, 1981.

Harper's Bible Commentary. Gen. ed. James L. Mays. San Francisco: Harper and Row, Publishers, 1988.

Harrison, Roland Kenneth. *Introduction to the Old Testament.* Grand Rapids: Eerdmans, 1969.

Hindson, Edward E. *The Philistines and the Old Testament.* Grand Rapids: Baker Book House, 1971.

Houston, Drusilla Dunjee Houston. *Wonderful Ethiopians of the Ancient Cushite Empire.* Baltimore: Black Classic Press, 1985.

_____. "Ethiopians in Old Arabia." In *African Presence in Early Asia.* Rev. ed. New Brunswick: Transaction Books, 1988.

Horizon History of Africa, ed. by Alvin M. Josephy, Jr. New York: American Heritage Publshing Co., Inc., 1971.

Hyman, Mark. *Blacks Who Died for Jesus.* Philadelphia: Corrective Black History Books, 1983.

Illustrated Bible Dictionary. (1980) Wheaton: Inter-Varsity Press. See specific articles.

International Dictionary of Biblical Archaeology, The New, ed. by E. M. Blaiklock, R. K. Harrison. Grand Rapids: Zondervan Publishing House, Regency Reference Library, 1983. See specific articles.

International Standard Bible Encyclopedia. (1979-1988) Grand Rapids: Eerdmans. See specific articles.

Jackson, John G. *Ethiopia and the Origin of Civilization.* Baltimore: Black Classic Press, 1939.

_____. *Man, God, and Civilization.* Secaucus: Citadel Press, 1972.

_____. *Was Jesus Christ A Negro? and The African Origin of the Myths and Legends of the Garden of Eden*, ed. by E. Curtis Alexander. Chesapeake, VA: ECA Associates, 1987 (1933).

_____. *Introduction to African Civilizations.* Secaucus, NJ: The Citadel Press, 1970.

Johnson, Johnnie L. *The Black Biblical Heritage.* St. Louis: The Black Biblical Heritage Publishing Company, 1975.

Josephus, Flavius. *The Works of Flavius Josephus: The Wars of the Jews; The Life of Flavius Josephus; Antiquities of the Jews.* 4 vols. Translated by William Whiston. Grand Rapids: Baker Book House, 1974.

Kessler, David. *The Falashas: The Forgotten Jews of Ethiopia.* New York: Schocken Books, 1985.

Kitchen, K. A. *Ancient Orient and Old Testament.* Wheaton: Inter-Varsity Press, 1966.

Ladson, Etta May. *Consecrated Captives: The Meaning of African Americans in America.* Laurelton, NY: Four Winds Press Publishers, 1987.

Lawson, Bishop R. C. *The Anthropology of Jesus Christ our Kinsman.* By the Author. New York, 1925.

_____. *An Open Letter to a Southern White Minister on Prejudice.* By the Author. ca. 1949.

Leupold, H.C. *Expositions of Genesis.* 2 vols. Grand Rapids: Baker Book House, 1942.

Livingston, G. Herbert. *The Pentateuch in Its Cultural Environment.* Grand Rapids: Baker Book House, 1974.

Matthews, Victor H. *Manners and Customs in the Bible.* Peabody, MA: Hendrickson Publishers, 1988.

McCray, Walter Arthur. *The Black Presence in the Bible and the Table of Nations (Genesis 10:1-32): With emphasis on the Hamitic Genealogical Line from a Black Perspective.* Chicago: Black Light Fellowship, 1990.

_____. *The Black Presence in the Bible: Discovering the Black and African Identity of Biblical Persons and Nations (Teacher's Guide).* Chicago: Black Light Fellowship, 1990.

_____. *A Rationale for Black Christian Literature.* Chicago: National Black Christian Students Conference, 1985.

_____. *Who Says God Says?! A Black Perspective Examining the Authority of New Testament Exegesis by Highlighting the Foundation for Its Interpretations and Applications.* Chicago: Black Light Fellowship, 1980.

McKissic, William Dwight, Sr. *Beyond Roots: In Search of Blacks in the Bible.* Wenonah, N.J.: Renaissance Productions, 1990.

Means, Sterling M. *Black Egypt and Her Negro Pharaohs.* Baltimore: Black Classic Press, 1945, 1978.

Meeks, Wayne A. *The First Urban Christians: The Social World of the Apostle Paul.* New Haven: Yale University Press, 1983.

Merrill, Eugene H. Merrill. *Kingdom of Priests: A History of Old Testament Israel.* Grand Rapids: Baker Book House, 1987.

Merrill, Reverend Richard. *The Curse of Canaan Resolved.* By the Author, 1978, 1981.

Morris, Henry M. *The Genesis Record: A scientific and devotional commentary on the book of beginnings.* Grand Rapids: Baker Book House, 1976.

Mosely, William. *What Color Was Jesus?* Chicago: African American Images, 1987.

New Bible Commentary: Revised, ed. by D. Guthrie, J. A. Moyer. Grand Rapids: Wm. B. Eerdmans Publishing Co., 1970.

New Bible Dictionary. 1982 ed. Wheaton: Tyndale House Publishers. See specific articles.

Newsome, James D., Jr. *A Synoptic Harmony of Samuel, Kings, and Chronicles.* Grand Rapids, Baker Book House, 1986.

Pritchard, James B. ed. *The Ancient Near East: An Anthology of Texts and Pictures.* vol. 1. *The Ancient Near East: A New Anthology of Texts and Pictures.* vol. 2. Princeton: Princeton University Press, 1958, 1975.

Rand McNally Contemporary World Atlas. Chicago: Rand McNally and Company, 1986.

Random House Dictionary of the English Language. 2nd ed. unabrid. New York: Random House, 1987.

Rashidi, Runoko. "Africans in Early Asian Civilizations: A Historical Overview," "People of the First World: Small Blacks in Africa and Asia," "More Light on Sumer, Elam and India," "The Blackheads of Sumer: A Bibliography." All in *African Presence in Early Asia.* Rev. ed. New Brunswick: Transaction Books, 1988.

_____. "The Nile Valley Presence in Asian Antiquity." In *Nile Valley Civilizations*, ed. by Ivan Van Sertima. New Brunswick: Journal of African Civilizations, 1985.

Rasmussen, Carl G. *Zondervan NIV Atlas of the Bible.* Grand Rapids: Zondervan Publishing House, Regency Reference Library, 1989.

Rhoades, Rev. Dr. F.S. *Black Characters and References of the Holy Bible.*

Rogers, J.A. *Sex and Race.* 3 vols. St. Petersburg: Helga M. Rogers, 1967. By the Author. 1980.

_____. *The Real Facts About Ethiopia.* Baltimore: Black Classic Press, 1936.

_____. *Nature Knows No Color-Line.* St. Petersburg: Helga M. Rogers, 1952, 1980.

_____. *As Nature Leads.* Baltimore: Black Classic Press, 1919, 1987.

_____. *World's Great Men of Color.* 2 vols. ed. by John Henrik Clarke. New York: Collier Books, Macmillan Publishing Company, 1972.

_____. *Africa's Gift to America.* St. Petersburg: Helga M. Rogers. 1961.

Rogerson, John. *Atlas of the Bible.* New York: Facts on File, 1986.

Ross, Allen P. *Creation and Blessing: A guide to the study and exposition of Genesis.* Grand Rapids: Baker Book House, 1988.

Schoville, Keith N. *Biblical Archaeology in Focus.* Grand Rapids: Baker Book House, 1978.

Smith, Rodney. *In the Land of Light: Israel, a Portrait of Its People.* Boston: Houghton Mifflin Company, 1983.

Snowden, Frank M. *Blacks in Antiquity.* Cambridge: Belknap Press, 1970.

Taryor, Kwiawon, Sr. *The Impact of the African Tradition on African Christianity.* Chicago: The Strugglers Press, 1984.

The Bible; *King James Version, Revised Standard Version, New International Version.*

Tierney, John., Wright, Lynda., Springen, Karen. "The Search for Adam & Eve: Scientists Explore a Controversial Theory About Man's Origins." *Newsweek,* January 11, 1988.

Tyndale Old Testament Commentaries. 24 vols. Gen. ed. D. J. Wiseman. Downer's Grove, IL: Inter-Varsity Press, 1973.

Unger, Merrill F. *The New Unger's Bible Dictionary,* ed. by R. K. Harrison. (1988 ed.) Chicago: Moody Bible Institute. See specific articles.

_____. *The New Unger's Bible Handbook.* Rev. by Gary N. Larson. Chicago: Moody Bible Institute, 1984.

Van Sertima, Ivan. "Editorial." In *Nile Valley Civilizations.* New Brunswick: Journal of African Civilizations, 1986.

_____. *The African Presence in Ancient America, They Came Before Columbus.* New York: Random House, 1976.

_____. ed. *African Presence in Early America.* New Brunswick: Transaction Books, 1987.

_____. ed. *African Presence in Early Europe.* New Brunswick: Transaction Books, 1988.

_____; Rashidi, Runoko, eds. "Editorial" in *African Presence in Early Asia.* New Brunswick: Transaction Books, 1988.

_____. ed. *Egypt Revisited.* New Brunswick: Transaction Publishers, 1989.

Walton, John H. *Ancient Israelite Literature in its Cultural Context: A Survey of Parallels between Biblical and Ancient Near Eastern Texts.* Grand Rapids: Zondervan Publishing House, 1989.

_____. *Chronological and Background Charts of the Old Testament.* Grand Rapids: Zondervan Publishing House, Academie Books, 1978.

Webb, James Morris, A.M. *The Black Man: The Father of Civilization. Proven by Biblical History.* San Francisco: Julian Richardson Associates, Publishers, ca. 1900.

Wenham, Gordon J. *Word Biblical Commentary: Genesis 1-15.* Waco: Word Books, 1987

Westermann, Claus. *Genesis 1-11: A Commentary.* Translated by John J. Scullion S.J. Minneapolis: Augsburg Publishing House.

Williams, Chancellor. *The Destruction of Black Civilization: Great Issues of A Race fromn 4500 B.C. to 2000 A.D.* Chicago: Third World Press, 1976.

Williams, Father Clarence. Exec. Prod. *"Search: The Black People's Presence In The Bible."* Detroit: Search, 1987.

Windsor, Rudolph R. *From Babylon to Timbuktu.* Smithtown: Exposition Press, 1969.

_____. *The Valley of the Dry Bones: The Conditions that Face Black People in America.* Philadelphia: Windor's Golden Series, 1986.

Wycliffe Bible Commentary, ed. by Charles F. Pfeiffer, Everett F. Harrison. Chicago: Moody Bible Institute, 1962.

Zondervan Pictorial Encyclopedia of the Bible. (1975) Grand Rapids: Zondervan. See specific articles.

Topical Index

C

Biblical Index

BLACK LIGHT FELLOWSHIP

A Beacon for the Black Community

312.722.1441

P.O. Box 5369
Chicago, IL. 60680
2859 W. Wilcox St.
Chicago, IL. 60612

The Black Presence in the Bible: Discovering the Black and African Identity of Biblical Persons and Nations *(Vol. 1)*
ISBN 0-933176-12-0   **$19.95**

The Black Presence in the Bible and the Table of Nations (Genesis 10:1-32) With emphasis on the Hamitic Genealogical Line from a Black Perspective. *(Vol. 2)*
ISBN 0-933176-13-9   **$19.95**

NAME _____

CH./ORG./BUS. _____

ADDRESS _____

CITY _____ ST _____ ZIP _____

PHONES (D) (___) _____ (E) (___) _____

The Black Presence in the Bible (Vol. 1)
                    ___ copies x **19.95** _____
The Black Presence in the Bible (Vol. 2)
                    ___ copies x **19.95** _____

    Shipping & Handling = $2.25 + .50/each add. _____

    TOTAL ENCLOSED (Check/M.O.) $_____

VISA/MASTER # _____ Expiration Date _____

Signature _____

Mail to: **Black Light Fellowship, P.O. Box 5369, Chicago, IL 60680**

(312) 722-1441   050591